Recipes: The Cooking of the British Isles

Contents

Foods of the World

TIME-LIFE BOOKS, ALEXANDRIA, VIRGINIA

Preserves

How to Prepare and Seal Canning Jars

To ensure consistent results in home canning, use standard canning jars with matching lids and rings; jams and jellies can be put up in jelly glasses with matching lids. An airtight seal is imperative. Examine each container carefully and discard those with covers that do not fit securely or those with cracked or chipped edges.

Wash the jars, glasses, lids and rings in hot, soapy water and rinse them with scalding water. Place them in a large, deep pot and pour in sufficient hot water to submerge them completely. Bring to a boil over high heat. Then turn off the heat and let the pan stand while you finish cooking the food that you plan to can. The jars or glasses must be hot when the food is placed in them.

To be ready to seal jelly glasses, grate a 4-ounce bar of paraffin into the top of a double boiler (preferably one with a pouring spout), and melt it over hot water. Do not let the paraffin get so hot that it begins to smoke; it will catch fire easily.

When food is ready for canning, remove the jars or glasses from the pot with tongs and stand them upright on a level surface. Leave canning lids and rings in the pot until you are ready to use them. Fill and seal the jars one at a time, filling each jar to within ⅛ inch of the top. Each jar should be sealed quickly and tightly with its ring and lid.

The jelly glasses, filled to within ½ inch of the top, should also be sealed at once. Pour a single thin layer of hot paraffin over the surface of jelly, making sure it covers the jelly completely and touches all sides of the glass. If air bubbles appear on the paraffin, prick them immediately with a fork or the tip of a knife. Let the glasses rest until the paraffin cools and hardens; then cover them with metal lids.

NOTE: If there is not enough food to fill the last jar or glass completely, do not attempt to seal it. Refrigerate and use it as soon as possible.

Apple Chutney

To make 3 pints

8 cups coarsely diced, peeled and
    cored green cooking apples (about
    3 pounds)
2 cups coarsely chopped onions
    (about 1 pound)
2 cups white seedless raisins
2 cups dark-brown sugar

1½ cups malt vinegar
1 tablespoon mustard seeds, crushed
    with a mortar and pestle or
    wrapped in a towel and crushed
    with a rolling pin
1½ teaspoons mixed pickling spice,
    tied in cheesecloth
½ teaspoon ground ginger
½ teaspoon cayenne pepper

In a heavy 6- to 8-quart enameled or stainless-steel pot, combine the apples, onions, raisins, brown sugar, vinegar, mustard seeds, pickling spice, ginger and cayenne pepper. Bring the mixture to a boil, stirring occasionally, then reduce the heat to low and simmer uncovered for 2 hours, or until most of the liquid has cooked away and the mixture is thick enough to hold its shape in a spoon. Stir it frequently as it begins to thicken, to prevent the chutney from sticking to the bottom and sides of the pan.

Remove the pot from the heat. With a large spoon, ladle the chutney immediately into hot sterilized jars, filling them to within ⅛ inch of the top and following the directions for canning and sealing *(opposite)*.

Green-Tomato Chutney

To make about 4 pints

9 cups coarsely diced unpeeled green
    tomatoes (about 3 pounds)
6 cups coarsely diced, peeled and
    cored green cooking apples (about
    2 pounds)
4½ cups coarsely chopped onions
    (about 1½ pounds)

2 cups coarsely diced celery, trimmed
    of all leaves (about ½ pound)
¾ cup seedless raisins
½ cup candied or preserved ginger
    (about 4 ounces), cut into ¼-
    inch dice
2 cups dark-brown sugar
1½ cups malt vinegar
1 tablespoon salt

In a heavy 6- to 8-quart enameled or stainless-steel pot, combine the green tomatoes, apples, onions, celery, raisins, ginger, brown sugar, vinegar and salt. Bring the mixture to a boil over high heat, stirring occasionally. Then reduce the heat to low. Simmer uncovered for 3 hours, or until most of the liquid has cooked away and the mixture is thick enough to hold its shape in a spoon. Stir it frequently as it begins to thicken, to prevent the chutney from sticking to the bottom and sides of the pan.

Remove the pot from the heat. With a large spoon, ladle the chutney immediately into hot sterilized jars, filling them to within ⅛ inch of the top and following the directions for canning and sealing *(opposite)*.

Bramble Jelly
To make about 4 cups

2 quarts fresh, ripe blackberries (about 3 pounds)

2 cups water
2½ cups sugar

Pick over the berries carefully, removing any stems and discarding fruit that is badly bruised or shows signs of mold. Do not discard any underripe berries; although tarter than ripe ones, they contain more pectin (the substance that jells the fruit), and a few will help ensure a firm jelly. Wash the berries in a colander under cold running water and drop them into an 8- to 10-quart pot. Add the 2 cups of water and bring to a boil over high heat. Reduce the heat to low and simmer uncovered for 1 hour, crushing the berries from time to time against the sides of the pot with a large spoon until the fruit becomes a coarse purée.

Line a colander or a sieve with protruding handles with 4 layers of dampened cheesecloth, and set it in another large pot. Pour in the berry purée. Allow the juice to drain through into the pot without disturbing it; squeezing the cheesecloth will make the final jelly cloudy.

When the juice has drained through completely, discard the berries and bring the juice to a boil over high heat. Boil the juice briskly, uncovered, until it is reduced to 3 cups, then add the sugar and cook, stirring until the sugar dissolves. Boil uncovered, without stirring, until the jelly reaches a temperature of 220° (or 8° above the boiling point of water in your locality) on a jelly, candy or deep-frying thermometer.

Remove the pot from the heat and carefully skim off all of the surface foam with a large spoon. Ladle the jelly immediately into hot sterilized jars or jelly glasses, filling them according to the directions for canning and sealing on page 2.

Red Currant Jelly
To make 3 cups jelly

2 quarts fresh ripe red currants (3 pounds)

3 cups water
2 to 3 cups sugar, preferably superfine

Pick over the currants carefully, removing the stems and discarding any fruit that is badly bruised or shows signs of mold. Do not discard any underripe berries; although more tart than ripe currants, they contain more pectin, the substance that causes the fruit to jell, and a few will ensure a firm jelly. Wash the currants in a colander under cold running water, then drop them into an 8- to 10-quart pot. Add the 3 cups of water and bring to a boil over high heat. Reduce the heat to moderate and cook uncovered for 30 minutes, stirring occasionally.

Set a colander or a sieve with protruding handles atop a large pot. Line the colander with 4 layers of dampened cheesecloth and pour in the currants. Allow the juice to drain into the pot without disturbing it; squeezing the cheesecloth will make the jelly cloudy.

When the juice has drained through completely, measure it and return it to the pot. Discard the currants. Add 1 cup of sugar for each cup of juice and bring to a boil over high heat, stirring until the sugar dissolves. Boil uncovered until the jelly reaches a temperature of 220° (or 8° above the boiling point of water in your locality) on a jelly, candy or deep-frying thermometer.

Remove the pot from the heat and carefully skim off and discard all the surface foam with a large spoon. Ladle the jelly into hot sterilized jars or jelly glasses, following the directions for canning and sealing on page 2.

NOTE: Red currant jelly is the traditional accompaniment for roast lamb and game.

Plum Jam
To make about 1 quart

4 pounds firm, ripe blue or red plums   4 pounds sugar (10 cups)

Wash the plums under cold running water and pat them dry with paper towels. Then cut them in half and pry out the pits. With a nutcracker or the tip of a knife, break open 12 of the pits and remove their kernels. Combine the plum halves and the 12 kernels in a 6- to 8-quart pot. Stir in the sugar.

Let the mixture rest at room temperature for 30 minutes, then set the pot over low heat and cook, stirring constantly with a wooden spoon, until the sugar dissolves. Bring to a boil over high heat, reduce the heat to moderate, and cook, stirring occasionally, for 45 minutes, or until the jam thickens and reaches a temperature of 221° (or 9° above the boiling point of water in your locality) on a jelly, candy or deep-frying thermometer. Remove from the heat. With a large spoon, carefully skim off the foam from the surface and ladle the jam into hot sterilized jars or jelly glasses, following the directions for canning and sealing on page 2.

Grapefruit Marmalade
To make about 4 pints

3 large, ripe grapefruit	8 to 10 cups sugar, preferably
2½ to 3 quarts cold water	superfine

Wash the grapefruit and pat dry with paper towels. With a knife or rotary peeler remove the skins without cutting into the bitter white pith. Cut the peel into strips about 1 inch long and ⅛ inch wide. Cut away and discard the white outer pith. Slice the fruit in half crosswise, wrap the halves one at a time in a double thickness of damp cheesecloth, and twist the cloth to squeeze the juice into a bowl. Wrap the squeezed pulp in the cheesecloth and tie securely. Add enough cold water to the bowl to make 3½ quarts of liquid. Drop in the bag of pulp and strips of peel. Let the mixture stand at room temperature for at least 12 hours.

Pour the entire contents of the bowl into an 8- to 10-quart stainless-steel or enameled pot, and bring to a boil over high heat. Reduce the heat to low and, stirring occasionally, simmer uncovered for 2 hours. Discard the bag of pulp and measure the mixture. Add 1 cup of sugar for each cup of mixture, stir thoroughly, and bring to a boil over moderate heat. When the sugar has dissolved, increase the heat to high and, stirring occasionally, boil briskly for about 30 minutes, until the marmalade reaches a temperature of 220° (or 8° above the boiling point of water in your locality) on a jelly, candy or deep-frying thermometer. Remove from the heat. With a large spoon, skim off the surface foam. Ladle the marmalade into hot sterilized jars or jelly glasses (*directions, page 2*). To prevent the peel from floating to the top, gently shake the jars occasionally as they cool.

Mincemeat

To make about 3 quarts

½ pound fresh beef suet, chopped
fine
4 cups seedless raisins
2 cups dried currants
1 cup coarsely chopped almonds
½ cup coarsely chopped candied
citron
½ cup coarsely chopped dried figs
½ cup coarsely chopped candied
orange peel
¼ cup coarsely chopped candied
lemon peel
4 cups coarsely chopped, peeled and
cored cooking apples
1¼ cups sugar
1 teaspoon ground nutmeg
1 teaspoon ground allspice
1 teaspoon ground cinnamon
½ teaspoon ground cloves
2½ cups brandy
1 cup pale dry sherry

Combine the suet, raisins, currants, almonds, citron, dried figs, candied orange peel, candied lemon peel, apples, sugar, nutmeg, allspice, cinnamon and cloves in a large mixing bowl and stir them together thoroughly. Pour in the brandy and sherry, and mix with a large wooden spoon until all the ingredients are well moistened. Cover the bowl and set the mincemeat aside in a cool place (not the refrigerator) for at least 3 weeks. Check the mincemeat once a week. As the liquid is absorbed by the fruit, replenish it with sherry and brandy, using about ¼ cup at a time. Mincemeat can be kept indefinitely in a covered container in a cool place, without refrigeration, but after a month or so you may refrigerate it if you like.

Vegetables and Pickles

Boxty Pancakes
IRISH POTATO PANCAKES

To make about 10 pancakes

3 medium-sized potatoes (about 1
   pound), preferably baking
   potatoes
½ cup flour
½ teaspoon salt

¼ cup milk
½ teaspoon caraway seeds (optional)
3 to 4 tablespoons butter or rendered
   bacon fat
Crisp fried bacon (optional)

Peel the potatoes and drop them into a bowl of cold water to prevent their discoloring. In a large bowl, stir together the flour, salt and milk, and optional caraway seeds. One at a time, pat the potatoes dry and grate them coarsely into a sieve or colander. As you proceed, press each potato firmly down into the sieve with the back of a large spoon to remove its moisture, then immediately stir the gratings into the flour-and-milk mixture.

In a heavy 8- to 10-inch skillet, melt 2 tablespoons of the butter or fat over moderate heat. When the foam begins to subside, pour in about 1 tablespoon of batter for each pancake. Cook 3 or 4 pancakes at a time, leaving enough space between them so that they can spread into 3½- to 4-inch cakes. Fry them for about 3 minutes on each side, or until they are golden brown and crisp around the edges. Transfer the finished pancakes to a heated plate and drape foil over them to keep them warm while you cook the remaining cakes, adding fat to the pan when necessary. Serve the pancakes as soon as they are all cooked, accompanied if you wish by crisp bacon.

Colcannon

MASHED POTATOES WITH CABBAGE AND SCALLIONS

To serve 4 to 6

6 medium-sized boiling potatoes
(about 2 pounds), peeled and
quartered
4 cups finely shredded green cabbage
(about 1 pound)
4 tablespoons butter
1 cup lukewarm milk

6 medium-sized scallions, including
2 inches of the green tops, cut
lengthwise in half and crosswise
into ⅛-inch slices
1 teaspoon salt
Freshly ground black pepper
1 tablespoon finely chopped fresh
parsley

Drop the quartered potatoes into enough lightly salted boiling water to cover them by 2 inches, and boil briskly until they are tender but not falling apart. Meanwhile, place the cabbage in a separate pot, pour in enough water to cover it completely, and bring to a boil. Boil rapidly, uncovered, for 10 minutes, then drain thoroughly in a colander. Melt 2 tablespoons of the butter over moderate heat in a heavy 8- to 10-inch skillet. When the foam begins to subside, add the cabbage, and cook, stirring constantly, for a minute or two. Cover the skillet and set aside off the heat.

Drain the potatoes and return them to the pan. Shake over low heat until they are dry and mealy. Then mash them to a smooth purée with a fork, a potato ricer or an electric mixer. Beat into them the remaining 2 tablespoons of butter and then ½ cup of the milk, 2 tablespoons at a time. Use up to ½ cup more milk if necessary to make a purée thick enough to hold its shape in a spoon. Stir in the cooked cabbage and the scallions, and add the salt and a few grindings of pepper. Taste for seasoning. Then transfer the colcannon to a heated serving bowl, sprinkle with parsley, and serve at once.

Game Chips
To serve 4 to 6

4 cups vegetable oil or shortening   (about 2 pounds), peeled
6 medium-sized baking potatoes   2 teaspoons salt

Preheat the oven to 250°. Line a jelly-roll pan or large, shallow roasting pan with a double thickness of paper towels, and set it aside. In a deep-fat fryer or large, heavy saucepan, heat the oil to 360° on a deep-frying thermometer, or until a haze forms above it.

With a large knife or a vegetable slicer, cut the potatoes into slices 1/16 inch thick and drop them directly into cold water to remove the starch and prevent them from discoloring. When ready to use, drain them in a colander, spread them out in a single layer on paper towels, and pat them thoroughly dry with more towels.

Drop about 1/2 cup of the potatoes at a time into the hot fat and, turning the slices about with a slotted spoon, fry for 2 or 3 minutes, or until they are crisp and golden brown. Transfer the chips to the paper-lined pan and keep them warm in the oven while you proceed with the remaining batches.

To serve, heap the chips in a heated bowl and sprinkle them with the salt. Game chips are traditionally served with roasted birds, such as pheasant (*Recipe Index*), in which case they may be arranged in a circle around the bird and served on the same platter.

Pease Pudding
PURÉED PEAS

To serve 6 to 8

                          1 teaspoon salt
2 cups dry green split peas (1 pound)   4 tablespoons butter
2 cups water   1/4 teaspoon white pepper

Wash the split peas thoroughly under cold running water and continue to wash until the draining water runs clear. Pick over the peas and discard any discolored ones. In a heavy 3- to 4-quart saucepan, bring the 2 cups of water to a boil and drop in the peas slowly so that the water continues to boil. Reduce the heat and simmer partially covered for 1½ hours, or until the peas can be easily mashed against the side of the pan with a spoon. Drain the peas in a colander and purée them in a food mill or force them through a fine sieve set over a large bowl. Return the peas to the pan and cook over low heat, stirring constantly, until the purée is heated through. Stir in the salt, butter and pepper, and taste for seasoning. Serve at once from a heated vegetable dish. Pease pudding is the traditional accompaniment to boiled beef and carrots with dumplings *(Recipe Index)*.

Pickled Onions

To make 2 pints

2 pounds white onions, each about 1 inch in diameter	½ cup sugar
	2 tablespoons mixed pickling spice
½ cup salt	5 whole cloves
1 quart malt vinegar	10 whole black peppercorns

To peel the onions easily, first drop them into a pot of boiling water and let them boil briskly for a minute or so. Then drain at once, pour cold water over them, and carefully remove their skins with the aid of a small, sharp knife. Place the onions in a large bowl, sprinkle them with ½ cup of salt, and turn them about with a spoon to coat them evenly. Cover the bowl and set aside in a cool place for at least 12 hours.

Drain the onions, wash them under cold running water, and pat them dry with paper towels. In a heavy 4- to 5-quart saucepan, bring the vinegar, sugar, pickling spice, cloves and peppercorns to a boil over high heat, stirring until the sugar dissolves. Boil briskly for 5 minutes, then add the onions. The liquid should cover the onions by ½ inch; if necessary add more water. Return to a boil, and cook briskly, uncovered, for 10 minutes, or until the onions show only slight resistance when pierced with the tip of a small, sharp knife. Do not overcook. With a slotted spoon, transfer the onions to hot sterilized jars, following the directions for canning and sealing on page 2. Pour the vinegar-and-spice mixture over them, filling the jars to within ¼ inch of the top. Seal at once.

As a further precaution against spoilage, finish the process with a water bath. Place the filled and sealed canning jars side by side on a rack in a canner or other large, deep pot. Pour in enough hot (not boiling) water to cover the jars by at least 1 inch, securely cover the pot with its lid, and bring to a boil over moderate heat. Boil for 5 minutes, then remove the jars from the pot with tongs.

Let the onions pickle at room temperature for at least 2 weeks before serving them.

Hot Mustard Pickle

To make about 3 quarts

1 medium-sized cauliflower (about
  1 pound), trimmed and separated
  into individual flowerets with
  approximately 1-inch stems
2 small green (unripe) tomatoes
  (about ½ pound), cut into 1-inch
  chunks
1 pound small white onions, about
  1 inch in diameter, peeled
2 medium-sized yellow onions
  (about ½ pound), peeled and cut
  into ¼-inch slices

1 cup plus 1 teaspoon salt
2 small cucumbers (about 1 pound),
  peeled and cut into ¼-inch slices
1 tablespoon capers, drained and
  rinsed in cold water
½ teaspoon celery seed
¼ pound butter
¼ cup all-purpose flour
2 cups malt vinegar
½ cup sugar
1 tablespoon turmeric
¼ cup dry English mustard

In a 10- to 12-quart enameled or stainless-steel pot, combine the cauliflower, green tomatoes, white onions and sliced yellow onions. Dissolve 1 cup of the salt in 4 quarts of water, pour it over the vegetables, and stir until they are thoroughly moistened. Set aside in a cool place (not the refrigerator) for 12 to 18 hours.

Drain off the liquid, and add the cucumbers, capers, celery seed, the remaining teaspoon of salt and 1 quart of fresh water to the pot. Bring to a boil over high heat, stirring occasionally. Then reduce the heat to moderate and cook, uncovered, for about 10 minutes, or until the vegetables are tender but still slightly resistant when pierced with the tip of a small knife. Drain through a colander, discard the liquid and place the vegetables in a large stainless-steel, glass or enameled bowl.

Melt the butter in a heavy 1½- to 2-quart saucepan over moderate heat. When the foam begins to subside, stir in the flour, and mix thoroughly. Pour in the vinegar and cook, stirring constantly, until the sauce thickens and comes to a boil. Reduce the heat to low and simmer for about 3 minutes, then beat in the sugar, turmeric and mustard. Pour half the sauce over the vegetables, turning them about to coat them evenly. Set the remaining sauce aside, covered with plastic wrap. (Do not refrigerate.) Marinate the vegetables at room temperature for 24 hours, then stir in the reserved mustard sauce. The pickles may be served at once, or packed into jars and stored, tightly covered, in the refrigerator for up to 3 months. Mustard pickle is traditionally served with cold meats or bread and cheese.

Pickled Cabbage

To make about 4 pints

2 medium-sized red cabbages (about 6 pounds)
6 tablespoons coarse (kosher) salt

1 quart malt vinegar
¼ cup sugar
2 tablespoons mixed pickling spice
1 teaspoon whole black peppercorns

Wash the cabbages under cold running water, remove the tough outer leaves, and cut each head into quarters. Shred the cabbage by first cutting out the cores and then slicing the quarters crosswise into ⅛-inch-thick strips. In a large stainless-steel or enameled bowl or pot, arrange the cabbage in 3 layers, sprinkling 2 tablespoons of coarse salt evenly over each layer. Let the cabbage stand in a cool place for 2 days, turning it about and lifting it up from the bottom of the bowl with a large wooden spoon several times each day.

On the third day, combine the vinegar, sugar, pickling spice and peppercorns in a 2- to 3-quart saucepan, and bring to a boil over high heat, stirring until the sugar dissolves. Boil briskly, uncovered, for 5 minutes, then remove the pan from the heat and cool to room temperature. Meanwhile drain the cabbage in a large colander. Squeeze it as dry as possible, a handful at a time, and return it to the bowl or pot. Strain the vinegar mixture over it, turning the cabbage about with a fork to moisten it thoroughly.

Cover, refrigerate, and let the cabbage marinate for at least 3 days before serving. Stir it occasionally. Covered tightly and refrigerated, it will keep for about 2 weeks.

Cheese

Glamorgan Sausages
FRIED CHEESE CROQUETTES

To make about 10 croquettes

2/3 cup freshly grated Cheddar cheese

2 cups fresh soft crumbs, made from homemade-type white bread, pulverized in a blender or shredded with a fork

2 tablespoons finely chopped scallions, including 1 inch of the green tops

1 tablespoon finely chopped fresh parsley

1/2 teaspoon dry English mustard

1/2 teaspoon salt

Freshly ground black pepper

2 egg yolks

2 tablespoons water

2 egg whites

4 tablespoons vegetable oil

In a large bowl, mix together the grated cheese, 1 cup of the bread crumbs, the scallions, parsley, mustard, salt and a few grindings of pepper. Add the egg yolks and water, and stir until the mixture can be gathered into a compact ball. If it crumbles, add more water, a few drops at a time, until the ingredients adhere. Divide the mixture into 10 equal portions and roll each one into a cylinder about 2½ inches long and ¾ inch in diameter.

One at a time, dip the rolls in the egg white and then in the remaining crumbs, lining them up side by side on a strip of wax paper as you proceed. In a heavy 10- to 12-inch skillet, heat the oil over high heat until it splutters. Add the rolls and cook, turning them gently with tongs or a spatula and regulating the heat so that they brown quickly and evenly without burning. Glamorgan sausages may be served as a lunch or supper dish.

Cheese Straws

CHEESE-FLAVORED PASTRY STICKS

To make about 30 sticks

4 tablespoons unsalted butter, chilled
   and cut into ¼-inch bits
4 tablespoons finely grated sharp
   Cheddar cheese

¾ cup all-purpose flour
⅛ teaspoon cayenne pepper
¼ teaspoon salt
1 egg yolk
2 tablespoons ice water

In a large, chilled mixing bowl, combine the butter, cheese, flour, cayenne pepper and salt. With your fingertips rub these ingredients together until they blend and look like flakes of coarse meal. Break up the egg yolk in a separate bowl with a fork, stir in the ice water, and pour over the flour mixture. Toss together until the ingredients are well mixed, then gather the dough into a compact ball, dust it lightly with flour and wrap it in wax paper. Refrigerate for at least 1 hour.

Preheat the oven to 400°. Place the ball of dough on a lightly floured surface and shape it into a rough rectangle about 1 inch thick. Dust a little flour over and under it, and roll it into a rectangle about 4 inches wide, 14 inches long and ¼ inch thick. With a pastry wheel or sharp knife, trim the edges neatly. Then cut the dough crosswise into strips about ½ inch wide and 4 inches long. Carefully transfer the strips to an ungreased baking sheet, and bake in the middle of the oven until the straws are firm and lightly colored. Do not let them brown too much. With a wide spatula, transfer the straws to a wire rack to cool before serving. Cheese straws will keep for up to two weeks refrigerated in tightly covered jars or tins.

Welsh Rabbit

To serve 2 to 4

4 slices homemade-type white bread, trimmed of crusts and toasted
2 cups (½ pound) freshly grated sharp Cheddar cheese combined with 1 tablespoon flour

¼ cup beer
1 tablespoon butter
1 teaspoon Worcestershire sauce
¼ teaspoon dry English mustard
A pinch of cayenne pepper
1 egg yolk

Arrange the slices of toast in 2 to 4 shallow ovenproof dishes just large enough to hold them comfortably, and set aside.

In a heavy 2- to 3-quart saucepan, combine the cheese-and-flour mixture, beer, butter, Worcestershire sauce, mustard and cayenne pepper. Cook over moderate heat, without letting the mixture boil. Stir constantly with a fork until the cheese has melted completely and the mixture is smooth. In a small bowl break up the egg yolk with a fork. Off the heat, stir it into the cheese and, when it is thoroughly absorbed, taste for seasoning and pour the rabbit evenly over the toast. Place the dishes under the broiler for a minute or two to brown the cheese lightly, and serve at once.

NOTE: The traditional name for this dish is Welsh rabbit, presumably a joking reference to the fact that cheese was often available when rabbits were not. In the late 18th Century, the dish came to be called Welsh rarebit, as it frequently still is, but rabbit is the correct designation.

Crowdie Cheese

COTTAGE CHEESE

To make about 1½ cups

4 rennet tablets
4 teaspoons cold water

2 quarts milk
4 tablespoons heavy cream
½ teaspoon salt

In a cup or small bowl, combine the rennet and water, stirring until the tablets dissolve. Slowly heat the milk in a 3- to 4-quart enameled or stainless-steel saucepan until it reaches a temperature of 98° to 100° on a candy thermometer, or until a drop sprinkled on your wrist feels neither warm nor cool. Remove the pan from the heat, stir in the rennet and set aside. In 5 to 10 minutes curds of cheese will have formed, surrounded by the watery liquid called whey. Pour the contents of the pan into a sieve lined with a double thickness of dampened cheesecloth and set over a bowl. Let the cheese drain undisturbed for 1½ hours, then discard the whey and transfer the curds to the bowl. With a table fork, stir in the cream and the salt, mashing the curds against the sides of the bowl until smooth. Serve the cheese at room temperature. Traditionally it is accompanied by oatcakes (*opposite*).

Breads, Buns and Cakes

Oatcakes

To serve 4

1¾ cups regular oatmeal
¼ teaspoon baking powder

½ teaspoon salt
1 tablespoon butter, melted
5 to 8 teaspoons hot water

Preheat the oven to 350°. Half a cup at a time, pulverize 1 cup of the oatmeal by blending at high speed in the jar of an electric blender. Combine the pulverized oatmeal, baking powder and salt in a bowl, and stir in the melted butter. When all the butter has been absorbed, add the hot water, a teaspoon at a time, stirring constantly, to make a smooth but firm paste.

Gather the mixture into a ball and place it on a board or table lightly sprinkled with ¼ cup of the remaining oatmeal. Roll the ball into the oatmeal until it is completely covered with the flakes. Spread another ¼ cup of oatmeal evenly over the board and, with a rolling pin, roll the ball out into an 8-inch circle about ⅛ inch thick. With a pastry wheel or sharp knife, cut the circle into 8 pie-shaped wedges. Scatter the remaining ¼ cup of oatmeal on a baking sheet and, with a large metal spatula, carefully transfer the wedges to the sheet.

Bake the cakes in the middle of the oven for about 15 minutes. When the wedges are light brown, turn off the heat and open the door of the oven. Leave the oatcakes in the oven for 4 or 5 minutes, or until they become firm and crisp. Serve at once.

In Scotland, oatcakes are traditionally buttered and served with herring or cheese, but they may be served, alternatively, with honey or jam.

Irish Soda Bread

To make one 8-inch round loaf

1 tablespoon butter, softened
4 cups all-purpose flour

1 teaspoon baking soda
1 teaspoon salt
1 to 1½ cups buttermilk

Preheat the oven to 425°. With a pastry brush coat a baking sheet evenly with the tablespoon of softened butter.

Sift the flour, soda and salt together into a deep mixing bowl. Gradually add 1 cup of the buttermilk, beating constantly with a large spoon until the dough is firm enough to be gathered into a ball. If the dough crumbles, beat up to ½ cup more buttermilk into it by the tablespoon until the particles adhere.

Place the dough on a lightly floured board, and pat and shape it into a flat circular loaf about 8 inches in diameter and 1½ inches thick. Set the loaf on the baking sheet. Then with the tip of a small knife, cut a ½-inch-deep X into the dough, dividing the top of the loaf into quarters.

Bake the bread in the middle of the oven for about 45 minutes, or until the top is golden brown. Serve at once.

Hot Cross Buns

To make about 2 dozen buns

2 packages active dry yeast
2 tablespoons sugar
½ cup lukewarm milk (110° to 115°), plus 1 cup milk
3½ to 4½ cups all-purpose flour
½ teaspoon salt
1 teaspoon ground allspice

1 teaspoon ground cinnamon
2 eggs
4 tablespoons unsalted butter, softened
⅔ cup white raisins
1 lightly beaten egg combined with 1 tablespoon heavy cream

In a small shallow bowl, sprinkle the yeast and sugar over the lukewarm milk. Let the mixture stand for 2 or 3 minutes, then stir it to dissolve the yeast completely. Set the bowl in a warm, draft-free place, such as an unlighted oven, for 5 to 8 minutes, or until the yeast bubbles up and the mixture almost doubles in volume.

Sift 3½ cups of the flour, the salt, allspice and cinnamon into a deep mixing bowl. Make a well in the center and pour in the yeast mixture and the remaining cup of milk. Drop in the eggs and beat with a large spoon until the flour is absorbed. Beat in 3 tablespoons of the softened butter cut into bits, then add up to 1 cup more flour, a few tablespoons at a time, using only as much as necessary to make a dough that can be gathered into a soft ball.

When the dough becomes too stiff to stir easily, work in the additional flour with your fingers.

On a lightly floured surface, knead the dough by folding it end to end, then pressing it down and pushing it forward several times with the heel of your hand. Sprinkle the dough with a little extra flour when necessary to prevent it from sticking to the board. Repeat for about 10 minutes, or until the dough is smooth and elastic.

Shape the dough into a ball and place it in a large, lightly buttered bowl. Dust the top of the ball with a little flour, drape a kitchen towel over the bowl, and set in a warm, draft-free spot for 45 minutes to an hour, until the dough doubles in bulk.

With a pastry brush, coat a large baking sheet with the remaining tablespoon of softened butter. Punch the dough down with a single blow of your fist, then transfer it to a lightly floured board and knead the raisins into it. Pull off a small handful of the dough and set it aside.

For each bun, roll a small piece of the dough between your palms into a ball about 1½ inches in diameter. Arrange the balls about 2 inches apart on the baking sheet and set them aside to rise in the warm, draft-free place for about 15 to 20 minutes, or until they double in volume. Meanwhile preheat the oven to 450°.

With a small knife, cut a cross ⅓ inch deep on the top of each bun. Shape the reserved handful of dough into one or two long ropes about ¼ inch in diameter and cut it into strips 1½ inches long. Press the strips into the crosses on the top of the buns.

Brush the buns lightly with the egg-and-cream mixture, and bake in the middle of the oven for about 15 minutes, or until the tops are a deep golden brown. Transfer the buns to a cake rack and let them cool for a few minutes before separating them.

NOTE: If you prefer, you may make the cross on top of the buns with thin strips of candied orange peel instead of the strips of dough.

Crumpets
To make about 10 crumpets

1 package active dry yeast
½ teaspoon sugar
2 tablespoons lukewarm water (110°
    to 115°)
1 cup all-purpose flour

¼ teaspoon salt
½ cup milk
1 egg
5 tablespoons butter cut into ¼-
    inch bits

NOTE: To make traditional English crumpets, you will need five or six 3-inch round flan rings or open-topped cookie cutters. Substitute molds easily can be made, if necessary, by removing the tops and bottoms from five or six tin cans that are 3 inches in diameter and 1 to 2 inches tall, such as ordinary tuna cans.

In a small, shallow bowl, sprinkle the yeast and sugar over the 2 tablespoons of lukewarm water and let them stand for 2 or 3 minutes. Then stir them together to dissolve the yeast completely. Set the bowl in a warm, draft-free place, such as an unlighted oven, for 4 or 5 minutes, or until the yeast bubbles up and the mixture almost doubles in volume.

Sift the flour and salt into a large mixing bowl and make a well in the center. Pour in the yeast mixture and the milk, and drop in the egg. Beat vigorously with a large spoon, then add 1 tablespoon of the butter and beat until a smooth soft batter is formed. Drape a towel loosely over the bowl and set it aside in a warm draft-free place for about 1 hour, or until the batter has doubled in volume.

In a small pan, clarify the remaining 4 tablespoons of butter by melting it slowly without letting it brown. Skim off the surface foam and spoon the clear butter into a bowl, discarding the milky solids at the bottom of the pan. With a pastry brush, coat the bottom of a heavy 10- to 12-inch skillet and the inside surfaces of the flan rings or cookie cutters or cans with about half the clarified butter.

Arrange the rings in the skillet and place the pan over moderate heat. For each crumpet, drop about 1 tablespoon of batter into each ring. The batter will immediately spread out and fill the ring. When the crumpets begin to bubble and their bottoms turn a light brown remove the rings. Turn the crumpets over with a wide spatula and cook for another minute or so to brown them on the other side. Transfer the crumpets to a heated serving plate and cover with foil to keep them warm while you coat the skillet and rings with the rest of the clarified butter and cook the remaining batter.

Crumpets are traditionally served at breakfast and at afternoon tea. Accompany them with unsalted butter, syrups and your choice of jams, jellies or marmalades.

Shortbread

To make about 2 dozen triangles

1 tablespoon plus 1 pound (4 sticks) unsalted butter, softened

1 cup superfine sugar

5 cups all-purpose flour, sifted before measuring

Preheat the oven to 350°. Using a pastry brush, coat a large baking sheet with 1 tablespoon of the softened butter. Set aside.

With an electric mixer, beat the 1 pound of butter and the cup of sugar together at high speed until the mixture is light and fluffy. Then reduce the speed to medium and beat in the flour, a cup at a time; continue beating until the mixture is smooth. (To make the dough by hand, cream the 1 pound of butter and the sugar together by beating and mashing them against the sides of a mixing bowl with a large spoon until the mixture becomes fluffy. Add the flour, a cup at a time, beating well after each addition. If the dough becomes stiff to stir, knead in the remaining flour with your hands.)

On a lightly floured surface, roll the dough into a rectangle roughly 10 inches long by 8 inches wide and about ½ inch thick. With a ruler and a pastry wheel or a small, sharp knife, cut the rectangle lengthwise into four 2-inch-wide strips, and make crisscrossing diagonal cuts at 2½-inch intervals across them to form small triangles. Prick the pieces all over with the tines of a fork, making an even pattern of tiny holes on the surface. Arrange the triangles on the baking sheet and bake in the middle of the oven for 25 to 30 minutes, or until firm to the touch and delicately browned. With a wide metal spatula, transfer the triangles to cake racks to cool completely. Shortbread will keep for 2 or 3 weeks in tightly covered jars or tins.

NOTE: Shortbread dough may be baked in various shapes. Sometimes it is rolled and cut into rectangular cookies; sometimes it is rolled out into one large round cake and the surface marked with a knife tip so that it can be divided into individual wedges.

Parkin Biscuits

To make about 12 three-inch cookies

1 tablespoon butter, softened, plus
    2 tablespoons butter, chilled and
    cut into ¼-inch pieces
½ cup all-purpose flour
¼ cup sugar
¼ cup regular oatmeal
½ teaspoon baking soda
¼ teaspoon ground ginger
¼ teaspoon ground cinnamon
3 tablespoons imported English
    golden syrup, or substitute 3
    tablespoons dark corn syrup
1 egg, lightly beaten
6 whole blanched almonds, split in
    half

Preheat the oven to 350°. Using a pastry brush, coat a large baking sheet with the tablespoon of softened butter. Set aside.

In a large chilled bowl, combine the flour, sugar, oatmeal, baking soda, ginger and cinnamon. Stir them together, then add the 2 tablespoons of chilled butter. With your fingertips, rub the flour and butter together until they look like flakes of coarse meal. Warm the syrup for a few minutes over low heat until it runs easily off a spoon. Cool slightly, then slowly stir in the beaten egg and pour over the flour mixture. Beat with a wooden spoon until a pastelike dough is formed.

For each cookie, drop a heaping tablespoon of the dough on the baking sheet, and press an almond half into the center of each. Place the cookies about 2 inches apart. Bake in the middle of the oven for about 10 minutes, or until the cookies are firm to the touch and light brown. Slide them onto a cake rack to cool. The parkin biscuits will keep as long as 2 weeks in a tightly covered jar or tin.

Eccles Cakes

To make about 12 cakes

1 tablespoon butter, softened, plus
    2 tablespoons butter, melted
3 tablespoons sugar
½ cup dried currants
1 tablespoon finely chopped mixed
    candied fruit peel
⅛ teaspoon ground allspice
⅛ teaspoon ground nutmeg
Short-crust pastry *(page 76)*
Superfine sugar

Preheat the oven to 475°. Using a pastry brush, coat a large baking sheet with 1 tablespoon of softened butter. Set aside. In a small bowl, combine the melted butter and the 3 tablespoons of sugar, and stir in the currants, candied fruit peel, allspice and nutmeg. Toss the fruit about with a spoon until it is evenly coated.

On a lightly floured board, roll the pastry into a circle about ¼ inch

22

thick. With a cookie cutter or the rim of a glass, cut it into 3½-inch rounds. Gather the scraps together into a ball, roll it out into another circle, and cut out rounds as before.

Place a heaped tablespoon of the fruit mixture in the center of each round. Then bring up the outside edges of the pastry and twist together to enclose the filling. Turn over, and with the rolling pin press them gently but firmly into flat rounds. The currants should be just visible below the surface of the rounds. With the tip of a small, sharp knife make crisscrossing slits about 2 inches long in the center of each cake.

Place the cakes on the baking sheet and bake in the middle of the oven for about 15 minutes, or until they are golden brown. With a wide metal spatula, transfer the cakes to a rack to cool. Just before serving, sprinkle each cake generously with superfine sugar.

Eccles cakes are traditionally served at afternoon tea. They will keep for 1 to 2 weeks in a tightly covered jar or tin.

Rich Tea Scones

To make about 12 scones

1 tablespoon butter, softened
2 cups all-purpose flour
2 teaspoons baking powder
¼ cup sugar
1 teaspoon salt

6 tablespoons butter, cut into ¼-inch
   bits and thoroughly chilled
1 egg
1 egg yolk
½ cup milk
1 egg white

Preheat the oven to 400°. Using a pastry brush, coat a large baking sheet with the softened butter and set it aside.

Sift the flour, baking powder, sugar and salt together into a large chilled mixing bowl. Add the butter bits and, with your fingertips, rub the flour mixture and butter together until they look like flakes of coarse meal. With a whisk or fork beat the egg and egg yolk together until they froth. Beat the milk into the egg mixture and pour it over the flour mixture. With your hands or a large spoon, toss together until the dough can be gathered into a compact ball. Dust lightly with flour and on a lightly floured surface roll the dough out into a ½-inch-thick circle. With a cookie cutter or the rim of a glass, cut the dough into 2-inch rounds. Reroll and cut the scraps into similar rounds. Place the rounds about 1 inch apart on the baking sheet. With a fork beat the egg white briskly and then brush it lightly over the tops of the rounds. Bake in the middle of the oven for 15 to 20 minutes, or until light brown. Serve at once on a heated platter.

Brandy Snaps

To make about 15 brandy snaps

8 tablespoons (1 stick) unsalted
    butter, softened
⅓ cup confectioners' sugar
4 tablespoons imported English
    golden syrup, or substitute 10
    teaspoons light corn syrup
    combined with 2 teaspoons
    molasses

½ cup all-purpose flour
½ teaspoon ground ginger
2 tablespoons brandy
2 teaspoons finely grated lemon peel

FILLING
1½ cups heavy cream
¼ cup confectioners' sugar
2 tablespoons brandy

Preheat the oven to 350°. Use a pastry brush to coat a large baking sheet with 1 tablespoon of softened butter and then coat the handle of a long wooden spoon with another tablespoon of butter. Set aside.

In a heavy 10- to 12-inch skillet, bring 4 tablespoons of the butter, ⅓ cup of sugar and the syrup to a boil over moderate heat, stirring until the butter melts and the sugar dissolves. Remove the pan from the heat. With a large spoon gradually beat in the flour, ginger, brandy and lemon peel. Continue to beat until smooth. Let cool slightly for 2 or 3 minutes. Drop the batter by the teaspoonful onto the baking sheet, spacing the cookies about 4 inches apart. Bake in the middle of the oven for 5 to 8 minutes, or until the cookies have spread into 3- to 4-inch rounds and have turned a golden brown. Remove the cookie sheet from the oven and let it stand on a rack for 1 or 2 minutes, or until the cookies hold their shape when a spatula is slipped under them. If the cookies cool too much, they will harden and it will be difficult to shape them.

Working quickly, remove one cookie at a time with a metal spatula and roll it into a tube around the butter-coated handle of the spoon. Slide the tube off the handle onto a cake rack and proceed in the same fashion with the other cookies. Use the remaining butter to keep the spoon handle coated.

Just before serving, beat the cream in a chilled bowl with a whisk or a rotary or electric beater until it thickens slightly. Add ¼ cup of sugar and continue to beat until the cream forms stiff peaks on the beater when it is lifted out of the bowl. With a rubber spatula, gently but thoroughly fold in the brandy. Fill a pastry bag with the brandied cream and pipe it into the brandy snaps. Serve at once.

Maids of Honor
ALMOND TARTS

To make about 18 tarts

2 tablespoons butter, softened
5 tablespoons flour
Short-crust pastry *(page 76)*
2 egg yolks
½ cup sugar

½ cup blanched almonds, pulverized
   in a blender or with a nut grinder
   or a mortar and pestle
1 tablespoon finely grated lemon
   peel
2 tablespoons heavy cream

Preheat the oven to 400°. With a pastry brush and the 2 tablespoons of softened butter, coat the inside surfaces of 2 medium-sized 12-cup muffin tins (each cup should be about 2½ inches across at the top). Sprinkle 4 tablespoons of the flour into the tins, tipping them to coat the bottoms and sides of the cups evenly. Then invert the tins and rap them sharply on a table to remove the excess flour.

On a lightly floured surface, roll the short-crust pastry into a circle about ¼ inch thick, and with a cookie cutter or the rim of a glass, cut it into 3-inch rounds. Gather the scraps together into a ball, roll it out into another circle, and cut out rounds as before. Gently fit the rounds into the cups of the muffin tins, pushing the pastry firmly into the sides. The pastry shells will be about 1 inch deep, and will not fill the cups completely.

In a mixing bowl, beat the egg yolks with a whisk to break them up. Then beat in the sugar, almonds, lemon peel and the remaining tablespoon of flour. Slowly add the cream and beat until the mixture is smooth. Ladle about 1 tablespoon of the mixture into each of the pastry shells, filling them to within ⅛ inch of the top.

Bake in the middle of the oven for 15 to 20 minutes, or until the filling is a light golden brown. Carefully remove the tarts from the tins and cool them to room temperature on cake racks. Maids of honor are traditionally served at afternoon tea.

NOTE: In some parts of England, jam or bread crumbs are added to the filling, and it is not uncommon to find the tarts topped with two crossed strips of the pastry.

Swiss Roll with Lemon-Curd Filling

To make one 17-inch roll

	4 eggs
2 tablespoons butter, softened	½ cup self-rising flour
2 tablespoons all-purpose flour	Lemon curd *(below)*
6 tablespoons sugar	2 tablespoons superfine sugar

Preheat the oven to 400°. Using a pastry brush, coat the bottom and sides of an 11-by-17-inch jelly-roll pan with 1 tablespoon of softened butter. Line the pan with a 22-inch-long strip of wax paper, and let the paper extend over the ends of the pan. Brush the remaining butter over the paper, and sprinkle 2 tablespoons of all-purpose flour over it, tipping the pan to spread the flour evenly. Invert the pan and rap it sharply to remove the excess.

With a whisk or a rotary or electric beater, beat the 6 tablespoons of sugar and the eggs together until the mixture is light and fluffy. A little at a time, sift the self-rising flour over the eggs, folding the mixture together gently but thoroughly with a rubber spatula. Do not overmix. Pour the batter into the jelly-roll pan and, with a spatula, spread it out evenly. Bake in the middle of the oven for 10 minutes, or until the top is a light golden color and the cake has begun to come away from the sides of the pan. Remove the cake from the oven and dust it evenly with the superfine sugar. Then turn it out on a sheet of wax paper and gently peel off the paper. Spread the top of the cake evenly with lemon curd and, starting at the long edge, roll it into a cylinder. Cool to room temperature. To serve, cut the cake into ½-inch slices and arrange the slices attractively on a plate.

Lemon Curd

To make about 1 cup

	½ cup fresh lemon juice
4 tablespoons unsalted butter	4 egg yolks
½ cup sugar	1 tablespoon grated lemon peel

In a heavy 1½- to 2-quart saucepan, combine the butter, sugar, lemon juice and egg yolks. Cook over the lowest possible heat, stirring constantly, until the mixture thickens enough to heavily coat the back of a spoon. Do not let the mixture boil or the egg yolks will curdle. Pour the curd into a small bowl and stir in the lemon peel. Refrigerate until ready to use. Lemon curd is used as a filling for tarts and cakes such as Swiss roll *(above)*.

Madeira Cake

To make one 9-inch loaf

1 tablespoon plus ½ pound (2 sticks) butter, softened
2 tablespoons plus 2 cups sifted all-purpose flour
1 cup plus 2 tablespoons sugar

5 eggs
1 teaspoon grated lemon peel
½ teaspoon double-acting baking powder
1 tablespoon mixed candied fruit peel

Preheat the oven to 350°. Using a pastry brush, coat the bottom and sides of a 9-by-5-by-3-inch loaf pan with 1 tablespoon of the softened butter. Sprinkle the pan with 2 tablespoons of the flour, tipping it from side to side to coat it evenly. Then invert the pan and rap it on a table to remove any excess. Set aside.

In a large bowl, cream the remaining ½ pound of butter and 1 cup of the sugar together by mashing and beating them against the sides of the bowl with a large spoon until light and fluffy. Then beat in the eggs, add the grated lemon peel, and continue beating until smooth. Combine the 2 cups of flour and the baking powder, and sift them into the egg-and-sugar mixture, ½ cup at a time, beating well after each addition.

Pour the batter into the prepared pan, smooth the top with a spatula, and bake in the middle of the oven for 30 minutes. Sprinkle the candied peel evenly over the cake, and dust the entire surface with the remaining 2 tablespoons of sugar. Return the pan to the oven and bake for 30 minutes longer, or until a cake tester inserted in the center comes out clean. Let the cake cool for 5 minutes before removing it from the pan. Then allow it to cool completely on a cake rack.

Madeira cake is served unfrosted, usually at afternoon tea. Its name derives from the traditional practice of serving it with a glass of Madeira.

Gingerbread

To make one 7-by-12-inch cake

1 tablespoon butter, softened
2½ cups all-purpose flour
1½ cups dark-brown sugar
1 tablespoon ground ginger
1 tablespoon ground cinnamon
1 teaspoon baking soda

¼ teaspoon salt
¼ pound plus 4 tablespoons (1½ sticks) unsalted butter
4 tablespoons dark molasses
4 tablespoons dark corn syrup
2 eggs

Preheat the oven to 350°. Using a pastry brush, coat the bottom and sides of a 7-by-12-by-2-inch baking dish or cake pan with 1 tablespoon of softened butter. Set aside.

Sift the flour, sugar, ginger, cinnamon, baking soda and salt together into a large bowl. In a heavy 2- to 3-quart saucepan combine the ¼ pound plus 4 tablespoons of unsalted butter, the molasses and the corn syrup, and bring to a simmer over low heat. Cook, stirring constantly, until the butter melts. Then pour it over the flour mixture in a thin stream, stirring constantly with a large spoon. When the batter is smooth, add the eggs one at a time, beating well after each addition.

Pour the batter into the buttered dish, and bake in the middle of the oven for about 25 minutes, or until a cake tester inserted in the center comes out clean. Cool and serve at room temperature.

Chocolate Cake with Hazelnuts

To make one 8-inch round cake

8 ounces shelled hazelnuts
½ pound unsweetened baking chocolate, grated fine
1 teaspoon butter, softened
¾ cup plus 2 tablespoons flour
½ pound unsalted butter (2 sticks), softened
1 cup plus 2 tablespoons superfine sugar
1 teaspoon vanilla extract
7 egg yolks
7 egg whites
A pinch of salt

Preheat the oven to 400°. Spread the hazelnuts in a baking pan and toast for 15 minutes, turning them occasionally. Remove the pan from the oven and reduce the heat to 250°. While the hazelnuts are hot, rub them between kitchen towels to remove the skins. Chop 1 cup of the nuts fine and set them aside. Pulverize the rest in a blender or with a nut grinder or mortar and pestle. Stir them together with the grated unsweetened chocolate.

With a pastry brush and 1 teaspoon of softened butter, coat the bottom and sides of an 8-inch springform cake pan. Sprinkle the pan with 2 tablespoons of the flour and tip it from side to side to coat it evenly. Then invert the pan and rap it sharply to remove the excess flour. Set aside.

Cream the remaining ½ pound of butter, 1 cup of sugar and 1 teaspoon of the flour by mashing and beating them against the sides of the bowl with a large spoon. Then add the vanilla and beat in the egg yolks, one at a time. Combine the remaining flour with the nut-and-chocolate mixture, and beat in the butter-and-sugar mixture, a few tablespoons at a time. Continue to beat until the batter is smooth.

Place the egg whites and a pinch of salt in a separate bowl and beat with a whisk or a rotary or electric beater until they form firm unwavering peaks on the beater when it is lifted from the bowl. With a rubber spatula, gently but thoroughly fold the egg whites into the batter, using an over-under cutting motion rather than a stirring motion. Pour the batter into the cake pan and sprinkle the top evenly with the remaining 2 tablespoons of sugar. Bake in the middle of the 250° oven for 1 hour and 15 minutes, or until the sugar on top forms a crisp crust. Let the cake cool for 5 minutes. Then remove the sides of the pan and slide the cake off the base to a rack to cool completely.

ICING

¾ cup sugar	chocolate, cut into small pieces
⅓ cup water	1 tablespoon strong, freshly brewed
7 ounces semisweet baking	coffee

To prepare the icing, combine ¾ cup of sugar with the water, semisweet chocolate and coffee in a heavy 1- to 1½-quart saucepan. Cook over moderate heat, stirring constantly, until the mixture is smooth. Do not let it boil. Set the icing aside to cool briefly. Then transfer the cake to a serving plate and immediately spread the top and sides with icing. While the icing is still soft, press the reserved chopped nuts into the sides of the cake.

Black Bun

To make one 8-inch cake

PASTRY

½ pound (2 sticks) unsalted butter,
  chilled and cut into ¼-inch bits

2½ cups all-purpose flour

6 to 8 tablespoons ice water

1 tablespoon butter, softened

In a large, chilled bowl, combine the ½ pound of chilled butter and 2½ cups of the flour and rub them together with your fingers until they look like flakes of coarse meal. Do not allow the mixture to become oily. Pour 6 tablespoons of ice water over the flour all at once; then shape the dough into a ball. If the dough crumbles, add more ice water by the teaspoonful until the particles adhere. Dust the pastry lightly with flour and wrap it in wax paper. Refrigerate for at least 2 hours.

Preheat the oven to 350°. With a pastry brush and 1 tablespoon of soft butter, coat the bottom and sides of a round baking dish about 8 inches in diameter and 3 inches deep.

FILLING

4 cups all-purpose flour

½ cup sugar

1 teaspoon baking soda

1 teaspoon ground cinnamon

½ teaspoon mace

⅛ teaspoon ground cloves

¼ teaspoon salt

½ teaspoon freshly ground black
  pepper

6 cups seedless raisins (about 2
  pounds)

6 cups white raisins (about 2
  pounds)

2 cups coarsely chopped blanched
  almonds (about 12 ounces)

1½ cups finely chopped, mixed
  candied fruit peel (about 8 ounces)

3 eggs

½ cup buttermilk

1 cup brandy

To make the filling, sift the 4 cups of flour, the sugar, baking soda, cinnamon, mace, cloves, salt and pepper together into a mixing bowl. Add the seedless raisins, white raisins, almonds and candied peel a cup or so at a time, tossing them constantly with a spoon until the fruit and nuts are coated with the flour. Beat the eggs until frothy, stir in the buttermilk and brandy, and pour the mixture over the flour and fruit. Stir until all the ingredients are well combined.

Break off about two thirds of the chilled dough and place it on a lightly floured board. Pat it into a flat circle about 1 inch thick, and roll it out into a circle 15 to 16 inches in diameter and about ¼ inch thick. Drape the pastry over the pin and unroll it loosely over the baking dish. Gently press it into the bottom and around the sides of the dish, being careful not to stretch it. With scissors or a sharp knife, trim off the excess dough around the rim, and spoon the filling into the dish. Then roll the remaining pastry into a circle 9 to 10 inches in diameter and unroll it over the top of the dish. Cut off the excess and seal the edges of the circle securely to the dish by crimping it with your fingers or by pressing it down firmly with the tines of a fork. With a fork, prick the pastry all over the surface and, with a small knife, cut two 1-inch-long parallel slits about ½ inch apart in the center.

Bake in the center of the oven for 1½ hours, then reduce the heat to 275° and bake for another 1½ hours, or until the top is golden brown. Cool and then cover tightly with foil or plastic wrap and let stand at room temperature for at least a week before serving. In Scotland this dish is traditionally served on New Year's Eve. (It will keep for 3 or 4 weeks.)

Seedcake

To make one 8-inch round cake

¼ pound (1 stick) plus 1 tablespoon butter, softened	A pinch of salt
	¾ cup sugar
2½ cups all-purpose flour	1 tablespoon caraway seeds
1 teaspoon double-acting baking powder	1 egg
	½ cup milk

Preheat the oven to 350°. With a pastry brush or paper towel coat the bottom and sides of an 8-inch round cake pan evenly with 1 tablespoon of the softened butter. Set the pan aside. Sift the flour, baking powder and salt together into a small bowl and set aside. In a large bowl, cream the ¼ pound of softened butter and the sugar together by mashing and beating them against the sides of the bowl with a spoon until they are light and fluffy. Beat in the caraway seeds and then the egg. Add the flour mixture, ½ cup at a time, beating well after each addition. When the mixture is smooth, beat in the milk and pour the batter into the prepared pan. Smooth the top with a spatula and bake in the middle of the oven for 45 minutes, or until a cake tester inserted in the center comes out clean. Let the cake rest for 5 minutes in the pan, turn it out on a cake rack, and cool completely.

Dundee Cake

To make one 8-inch round cake

1 tablespoon plus ½ pound butter,
  softened
2 tablespoons plus 2½ cups all-
  purpose flour
1 cup sugar
5 eggs
¾ cup dried currants
¾ cup seedless raisins
¾ cup coarsely chopped mixed
  candied fruit peel

8 candied cherries, cut in half
½ cup almonds, pulverized in a
  blender or with a nut grinder or
  mortar and pestle
2 tablespoons finely grated orange
  peel
A pinch of salt
1 teaspoon baking soda dissolved
  in 1 teaspoon milk
⅓ cup blanched almonds, split
  lengthwise into halves

Preheat the oven to 300°. Using a pastry brush, coat the bottom and sides of an 8-by-3-inch springform cake pan with 1 tablespoon of the softened butter. Sprinkle in 2 tablespoons of the flour, tipping the pan to spread the flour evenly. Invert the pan, and rap it sharply to remove the excess.

In a large mixing bowl, cream the remaining ½ pound of butter and the sugar together by mashing and beating them against the sides of the bowl with a spoon until they are light and fluffy. Beat in one of the eggs, then ½ cup of flour and so on alternately until all the eggs and the 2½ cups of flour have been added. Beat in the currants, raisins, candied peel, cherries, pulverized almonds, grated peel and salt, and continue beating until well combined. Stir in the dissolved soda, pour the batter into the pan, and arrange the split almonds on top in concentric circles. Bake in the middle of the oven for 1½ hours, or until a cake tester inserted in the center comes out clean. Let the cake cool in the pan for 4 or 5 minutes, then cool it thoroughly on a rack before serving.

Irish Christmas Cake

To make one 9-inch round white fruitcake

¾ pound (3 sticks) plus 2 tablespoons butter, softened

1¼ cups plus 2 tablespoons all-purpose flour

⅔ cup coarsely chopped candied cherries

1¼ cups seedless raisins

1¼ cups white raisins

1¼ cups dried currants

¼ cup finely chopped mixed candied fruit peel

2 tablespoons finely chopped candied angelica

1¼ cups sugar

7 eggs

1 teaspoon ground allspice

1 tablespoon salt

1 cup finely chopped walnuts

Preheat the oven to 275°. Using a pastry brush, coat the bottom and sides of a 9-by-3-inch springform cake pan with 2 tablespoons of the softened butter. Sprinkle 2 tablespoons of the flour into the pan, tip it from side to side to spread the flour evenly, then invert the pan and rap it sharply on the bottom to remove excess flour. Combine the cherries, seedless and white raisins, currants, candied peel and angelica in a bowl, add ¼ cup of the flour, and toss the fruit about with a spoon to coat the pieces evenly. Set aside.

In a large bowl, cream ¾ pound of softened butter and the sugar and 2 more tablespoons of the flour together by mashing and beating them against the sides of the bowl until they are light and fluffy. Beat in the eggs, one at a time, then slowly beat in the remaining flour, the allspice and the salt. Combine the nuts with the fruit mixture and add the mixture to the batter, about ½ cup at a time, beating well after each addition. Pour the batter into the prepared pan, spreading it out with a spatula. Bake in the middle of the oven for 2 hours, or until the top of the cake is light golden in color or a cake tester inserted in the center comes out clean. Cool the cake completely before removing it from the pan.

English Christmas Cake

To make one 12-inch round fruitcake

½ pound (2 sticks) plus 4 tablespoons butter, softened

2 cups finely chopped mixed candied fruit peel (about 10 ounces)

2 cups white raisins (about 10 ounces)

1½ cups dried currants (about 8 ounces)

1 cup seedless raisins (about 5 ounces)

½ cup candied cherries, cut in half (about 4 ounces)

½ cup finely chopped candied angelica (about 4 ounces)

2 cups all-purpose flour

½ teaspoon double-acting baking powder

½ teaspoon salt

1 cup dark-brown sugar

1 cup shelled almonds (about 6 ounces), pulverized in a blender or with a nut grinder or mortar and pestle

4 eggs

¼ cup pale dry sherry, rum or brandy

Preheat the oven to 275°. Using a pastry brush, coat the bottom and sides of a 12-by-3-inch springform cake pan with 2 tablespoons of the softened butter. Coat one side of a 20-inch strip of wax paper with 2 more tablespoons of softened butter, and fit the paper, greased side up, inside the pan.

In a large bowl, combine the fruit peel, white raisins, currants, seedless raisins, cherries and angelica. Sprinkle the fruit with ½ cup of the flour, tossing it about with a spoon to coat the pieces evenly. Set aside. Then sift the remaining 1½ cups of flour with the baking powder and salt. Set aside.

In another large bowl, cream the remaining ½ pound of butter with the brown sugar by mashing and beating them against the sides of the bowl until they are light and fluffy. Add the pulverized almonds, then beat in the eggs one at a time. Add the flour-and-baking-powder mixture, a half cup or so at a time, then beat the fruit mixture into the batter. Finally, add the sherry and pour the batter into the springform pan. It should come to no more than an inch from the top. If necessary, remove and discard any excess.

Bake in the middle of the oven for 2 hours, or until a cake tester inserted in the center of the cake comes out clean. Let the cake cool for about 30 minutes before removing the sides of the springform, then slip the cake off the bottom of the pan onto a cake rack to cool completely. Then carefully peel off the wax paper.

GLAZE

¼ cup red currant jelly *(page 4)*

Heat the currant jelly in a small saucepan over moderate heat until it reaches a temperature of 225° on a candy thermometer or is thick enough to coat a wooden spoon lightly. With a small metal spatula, spread the hot glaze evenly over the top and sides of the cake.

MARZIPAN

2 cups almond paste
1 teaspoon almond extract
½ teaspoon salt

1 cup light corn syrup
7 cups confectioners' sugar (2 pounds), sifted

To make the marzipan, use an electric mixer, preferably one equipped with a paddle. Crumble the almond paste in small pieces into the bowl, add the almond extract and ½ teaspoon of salt, and beat at medium speed until well blended. Gradually add the corn syrup in a thin stream, beating constantly until the mixture is smooth. Then beat in the 7 cups of confectioners' sugar, ½ cup at a time. As soon as the mixture becomes so stiff that it clogs the beater, knead in the remaining sugar with your hands. From time to time it will be necessary to soften the marzipan as you add the sugar by placing it on a surface and kneading it for a few minutes. Press the ball down, push it forward, and fold it back on itself, repeating the process as long as necessary to make it pliable.

On a clean surface, roll out half the marzipan into a circle about ½ inch thick. Using a 12-inch pan or plate as a pattern, cut a 12-inch disc out of the circle with a pastry wheel or small, sharp knife. Roll and cut the remaining marzipan into a 36-by-3-inch strip. Gently set the disc of marzipan on top of the cake and press it lightly into place. Wrap the strip of marzipan around the cake, pressing it gently to secure it. If the strip overlaps the top, fold the rim down lightly.

Wrap the cake in foil or plastic, and let it stand at room temperature for at least 48 hours before icing. The cake may be stored for longer periods; it improves with age, and can be kept for several months.

ICING

6 cups confectioners' sugar, sifted
4 egg whites

1 tablespoon strained fresh lemon juice
⅛ teaspoon salt

Just before serving, ice the cake. Combine the 6 cups of confectioners' sugar, egg whites, lemon juice and ⅛ teaspoon salt in a large mixing bowl. With a whisk or a rotary or electric beater, beat until the mixture is fluffy but firm enough to stand in soft peaks on the beater when it is lifted out of the bowl. With a small metal spatula, spread the icing evenly over the sides and top of the cake. Then decorate the cake to your taste with swirls of icing, fresh or artificial holly and artificial mistletoe, candied fruits, or even small china reindeer, people and houses.

Fish

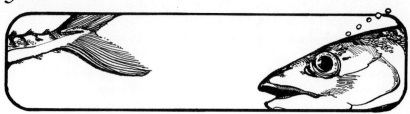

Mussel Brose
MUSSEL SOUP

To serve 4 to 6

3 dozen mussels in their shells
1 cup finely chopped leeks, including
   2 inches of the green
½ cup finely chopped celery
½ cup finely chopped onions
3 sprigs parsley
1 cup dry hard cider, preferably

imported English cider
3 tablespoons butter
3 tablespoons flour
2 cups milk
2 tablespoons heavy cream
Salt
Freshly ground black pepper
Ground nutmeg

Scrub the mussels thoroughly under cold running water with a stiff brush or soapless steel-mesh scouring pad. With a small, sharp knife scrape or pull the black ropelike tufts off the shells and discard them.

In a 6- to 8-quart enameled or stainless-steel pot, combine the leeks, celery, onions, parsley and cider. Drop in the mussels, cover, and bring to a boil over high heat. Reduce the heat to low and simmer for about 10 minutes, shaking the pot from time to time until the mussels open. Discard those that remain closed. With a slotted spoon transfer the mussels to a plate. Strain the stock through a fine sieve lined with a double thickness of cheesecloth, and return it to the pot.

Traditionally, the mussels are left in the half shell; to follow this method, remove and discard the upper half of each shell. Or you may remove the mussels from their shells entirely. In either case, cover the mussels with foil and set them aside. In a heavy 2- to 3-quart saucepan, melt the butter over moderate heat. Add the flour and mix together thoroughly. Pour in the milk and, stirring constantly with a whisk, bring to a boil over high heat. Reduce the heat to moderate and continue to cook, stirring, until the sauce is smooth and thick. Pour it into the strained stock, stir in the cream, and season lightly with salt and a few grindings of pepper and nutmeg.

Bring the soup to a simmer over low heat, stirring frequently. Then add the mussels and cook only long enough to heat them through. Taste for seasoning. Serve the soup from a heated tureen or individual soup plates.

Baked Stuffed Pike

To serve 4 to 6

3 tablespoons butter plus 2
    tablespoons butter, softened
½ cup finely chopped onions
1½ cups fresh soft crumbs, made
    from homemade-type white bread,
    pulverized in a blender or shredded
    with a fork
2 tablespoons finely chopped parsley
2 tablespoons milk
2 flat anchovy fillets, thoroughly
    drained and finely chopped
½ teaspoon finely grated lemon peel

1 teaspoon crumbled dried sage leaves
Salt
Freshly ground black pepper
1 large garlic clove, peeled and
    bruised with the flat side of a
    heavy knife
A 3-pound whole pike, cleaned and
    scaled but with head and tail left
    on, or substitute any other whole
    3-pound firm white fish
1 cup red Bordeaux or other dry
    red wine combined with ⅓ cup
    fresh orange juice

In a heavy 6- to 8-inch skillet, melt the 3 tablespoons of butter over moderate heat, add the onions and cook, stirring constantly, for 5 minutes, or until they are soft and transparent but not brown. With a rubber spatula, transfer them to a large mixing bowl, and stir in the bread crumbs, parsley, 2 tablespoons of milk, anchovy fillets, lemon peel, sage, ¼ teaspoon of salt and a few grindings of pepper. Taste for seasoning and set aside.

Preheat the oven to 350°. Rub the bruised garlic over the bottom and sides of a shallow baking-and-serving dish just large enough to hold the fish comfortably. Then with a pastry brush or paper towel, coat the bottom of the dish with 1 tablespoon of the softened butter.

Wash the fish inside and out under cold running water, and dry it thoroughly with paper towels. Loosely fill the cavity of the fish with the stuffing, then close the opening with small skewers, crisscrossing them with kitchen cord as if lacing a turkey. Brush the fish with the remaining tablespoon of softened butter and sprinkle it with salt and a few grindings of pepper. Place the fish in the baking dish, and pour in the combined wine and orange juice. Bake uncovered in the middle of the oven for 30 to 40 minutes, basting every 10 minutes with the pan liquid. The fish is done when its flesh is firm to the touch. Serve at once directly from the baking dish, moistening each serving with a little of the sauce.

Baked Mullet

To serve 2

3 tablespoons butter, softened
3 cups peeled, chopped fresh
   tomatoes, or substitute 3 cups
   finely chopped, drained canned
   tomatoes
12 large peeled shallots (about ¼
   pound)
2 tablespoons finely chopped parsley
1 teaspoon capers, drained and rinsed
   in cold water

1 teaspoon anchovy paste
1 teaspoon dry English mustard
2 whole 1-pound mullets, cleaned
   and scaled, but with heads and tails
   left on, or substitute any whole
   firm, white 1-pound fish
¼ teaspoon thyme
½ teaspoon salt
Freshly ground black pepper
1 teaspoon fresh lemon juice

Preheat the oven to 350°. With a pastry brush and 2 tablespoons of the butter, coat the bottom and sides of an 8-by-12-by-2-inch casserole or a baking
dish just large enough to hold the mullets comfortably.

In a heavy 2- to 3-quart saucepan, combine the chopped tomatoes, shallots, 1 tablespoon of the parsley, and the capers, anchovy paste and dry mustard. Bring to a boil over high heat, stirring constantly, then reduce the heat
to low, and simmer uncovered, stirring occasionally, for 10 minutes, or until
most of the liquid has evaporated and the sauce is thick. There should be
about 2 cups.

Meanwhile, wash the mullets inside and out under cold running water
and pat them thoroughly dry with paper towels. Lay the fish side by side in
the casserole and score the top of each fish with three parallel diagonal cuts
about an inch apart and ¼ inch deep. Sprinkle the fish evenly with the
thyme, salt and a few grindings of pepper, and spread the sauce over them.
Cover the dish and bake in the middle of the oven for 30 minutes, or until
the fish is firm to the touch. (Lacking a cover, a sheet of buttered foil will do
as well.)

With two wide metal spatulas, carefully transfer the fish to a heated serving platter. Remove the shallots from the sauce and strew them over the top.

With the aid of a rubber spatula, transfer the sauce remaining in the casserole to a small saucepan and briskly boil it over high heat, stirring
constantly, until it is reduced to about ½ cup. Remove the pan from the
heat, stir in the remaining 1 tablespoon of butter and 1 teaspoon of lemon
juice, taste for seasoning, and pour over the fish. Sprinkle with the remaining tablespoon of parsley and serve at once.

Fish and Chips

DEEP-FRIED FISH AND POTATOES

To serve 4

BATTER
1 cup flour
1 egg yolk
4 tablespoons beer

¼ teaspoon salt
6 tablespoons milk combined with 6
   tablespoons cold water
2 egg whites

To prepare the batter, pour the flour into a large mixing bowl, make a well in the center and add the egg yolk, beer and salt. Stir the ingredients together until they are well mixed, then gradually pour in the combined milk and water, and continue to stir until the batter is smooth.

For a light texture, let the batter rest at room temperature for at least 30 minutes, although if necessary it may be used at once. In either case, beat the egg whites until they form unwavering peaks on the beater when it is lifted from the bowl. Then gently but thoroughly fold them into the batter.

CHIPS
Vegetable oil or shortening for
   deep-fat frying

2 pounds baking potatoes, sliced
   lengthwise into strips ½ inch
   thick and ½ inch wide

To cook the chips and fish, heat 4 to 5 inches of oil or shortening in a deep-fat fryer to a temperature of 375° on a deep-fat-frying thermometer. Preheat the oven to 250°, and line a large shallow roasting pan with paper towels.

Dry the potatoes thoroughly and deep-fry them in 3 or 4 batches until they are crisp and light brown. Transfer them to the lined pan to drain and place them in the oven to keep warm.

FISH
2 pounds fresh, firm white fish fillets
   such as haddock, sole, flounder

or cod, skinned and cut into 3-by-
   5-inch serving pieces

Wash the pieces of fish under cold running water and pat them completely dry with paper towels. Drop 2 or 3 pieces of fish at a time into the batter and, when they are well coated, plunge them into the hot fat. Fry for 4 or 5 minutes, or until golden brown, turning the pieces occasionally with a spoon to prevent them from sticking together or to the pan.

To serve, heap the fish in the center of a large heated platter and arrange the chips around them. Traditionally, fish and chips are served sprinkled with malt vinegar and salt.

Poached Haddock with Parsley Sauce

To serve 4 to 6

A 3- to 4-pound whole fresh
haddock, cleaned and scaled, but
with head and tail left on, or
substitute any other 3- to 4-pound
whole firm, white fish
2½ quarts water

1 cup malt vinegar
1 tablespoon salt
1 teaspoon black peppercorns
¼ cup finely chopped fresh fennel
leaves or 1 tablespoon dried fennel
seed

Wash the fish inside and out under cold running water. Without drying it, wrap it in a long piece of damp cheesecloth of double thickness, leaving at least 6 inches of cloth at each end to serve as handles for lifting the fish. Twist the ends of the cloth and tie them with string. In a fish poacher or a deep covered roasting pan large enough to hold the fish comfortably, bring the water, vinegar, 1 tablespoon of salt, peppercorns and fennel to a boil over high heat.

Place the fish on the rack of the poacher or roasting pan, and lower it into the pan. The liquid should cover the fish by about 2 inches; add more boiling water if necessary. Cover, reduce the heat to its lowest point, and simmer slowly for 12 to 15 minutes, or until the fish feels firm when pressed lightly with a finger.

SAUCE
3 tablespoons butter
3 tablespoons flour
1½ cups milk

¼ cup finely chopped parsley
½ teaspoon salt
¼ teaspoon white pepper
1 tablespoon fresh lemon juice

Meanwhile, prepare the sauce. In a heavy 8- to 10-inch skillet, melt the butter over moderate heat. When the foam begins to subside, stir in the flour and mix thoroughly. Pour in the milk and, stirring constantly with a whisk, cook over high heat until the sauce thickens and comes to a boil. Reduce the heat to low and simmer for about 3 minutes to remove any taste of raw flour. Then add the parsley, ½ teaspoon of salt and white pepper. Just before serving, stir in the lemon juice and taste for seasoning.

Using the ends of the cheesecloth as handles, lift the fish from the pan and lay it on a large board or platter. Open the cheesecloth and skin the fish with a small, sharp knife by making a cut in the skin at the base of the tail and gently pulling off the skin in strips from tail to gill. Holding both ends of the cheesecloth, carefully lift the fish and turn it over onto a heated serving platter. Peel off the skin on the upturned side.

Serve the fish from the platter, the sauce from a separate bowl. If you like, you may debone the fish for serving. Divide the top layer into individual portions with a fish server without cutting through the spine. Leave the head and tail intact. Lift out the portions with the fish server and a fork, and arrange them attractively on another plate or platter. Then gently remove the backbone in one piece, discard it, and divide the bottom layer of fish into individual portions as before.

Soused Mackerel
To serve 6

3 one-pound mackerel, eviscerated, with heads removed but tails left on	1/8 teaspoon thyme
	12 whole black peppercorns
	1 1/2 teaspoons salt
2 medium-sized onions, thinly sliced and separated into rings	1 cup malt or white wine vinegar
	1 cup cold water
1/4 cup finely chopped parsley	2 tablespoons fresh lemon juice
2 small bay leaves	Parsley sprigs

Preheat the oven to 325°. Wash the mackerel inside and out under cold running water and pat them dry with paper towels. Lay the fish side by side in a shallow flameproof ceramic, stainless-steel or enameled baking pan just large enough to hold them comfortably. Strew the onion rings, chopped parsley and bay leaves evenly over the fish and sprinkle them with the thyme, peppercorns and salt. Pour in the vinegar, water and lemon juice, and bring to a boil over high heat. Then bake uncovered in the middle of the oven for 15 minutes, or until the fish are firm to the touch, basting them two or three times with the cooking liquid. Do not overcook. Let the fish cool to room temperature and cover tightly with foil or plastic wrap. Marinate in the refrigerator for at least 6 hours. Brush the onions and seasonings off the fish and, with a slotted spatula, carefully·transfer the mackerel to a platter.

To debone the mackerel for easier serving, divide the top layer into individual portions with a fish server without cutting through the spine. Leave the tail intact. Lift up the portions with the fish server and a fork, and arrange them on a serving dish. Lift out the backbone in one piece and divide the bottom layer of fish into portions. Garnish each serving with a sprig of parsley.

Kedgeree
CURRIED FINNAN HADDIE (FINDON HADDOCK) WITH RICE

To serve 2

3 tablespoons salt
1 cup long-grain rice
1 pound smoked haddock
4 tablespoons butter
1 tablespoon curry powder,

preferably imported Madras curry
powder
¼ teaspoon cayenne pepper
4 hard-cooked eggs, rubbed through
a sieve
2 tablespoons finely chopped parsley

Bring 6 quarts of water to a boil in a large heavy pot, add the salt, then pour in the rice in a thin, slow stream so that the water never stops boiling. Reduce the heat to moderate, and boil the rice uncovered for 15 minutes, or until the grains are tender but still slightly firm to the bite. Taste periodically to make certain.

Meanwhile, in a heavy 8- to 10-inch skillet, cover the haddock completely with cold water. Bring to a boil over high heat, reduce the heat to low and simmer uncovered for 10 minutes. With a slotted spatula transfer the fish to a plate and break it up into large flakes with a fork, discarding any bones you find. Cover and set aside.

In a heavy 3- to 4-quart saucepan, melt the butter over moderate heat. When the foam has almost subsided, sprinkle in the curry and cayenne pepper. Lower the heat and cook, stirring constantly, for about a minute. Then drain the rice in a colander and stir it into the butter with a fork. Add the flaked fish and return the saucepan to low heat.

Tossing the rice and fish together gently but thoroughly, cook for a minute or two, until the fish is heated through. Stir in half of the sieved eggs, and taste for seasoning. Transfer the kedgeree to a deep heated platter or a serving bowl, sprinkle with the remaining sieved eggs and the parsley, and serve at once.

Finnan Haddie
To serve 4

1 small onion, cut into ⅛-inch slices
and separated into rings
1 teaspoon whole black peppercorns

2 pounds smoked haddock, cut into
4 pieces
3 cups milk
Mustard sauce *(page 93)*

Strew the onion rings and peppercorns over the bottom of a heavy 10-inch skillet, and arrange the pieces of smoked haddock on top. Pour in the milk. The milk should just cover the fish; add more if necessary. Bring to a boil over high heat, then reduce the heat to low. Cover and simmer undisturbed for about 10 minutes, or until the fish flakes easily when prodded with a fork. Do not overcook.

With a slotted spatula, transfer the fish to a heated serving platter and discard the milk, onions and peppercorns. Serve the Finnan haddie at once, accompanied by a bowl of mustard sauce.

Jellied Eel
To serve 3 to 4

3 pounds eel, peeled, cleaned and cut into 2-inch pieces
2 tablespoons coarse salt
2½ cups water
¼ cup malt vinegar
1 medium-sized onion, peeled and thinly sliced

12 whole black peppercorns, wrapped in a cheesecloth packet and tied
2 small bay leaves
2 teaspoons salt
¼ cup fresh lemon juice
2 tablespoons finely chopped parsley
2 hard-cooked eggs, cut crosswise into ¼-inch slices

Wash the pieces of eel thoroughly under cold running water and arrange them in one layer in a shallow pan. Sprinkle evenly with the coarse salt, and pour in enough boiling water to cover the pieces completely. Soak for 5 minutes, then drain and rinse the pieces thoroughly under cold running water.

Place the eel in a heavy 4- to 5-quart stainless-steel or enameled saucepan. Add the water, vinegar, sliced onion, peppercorns, bay leaves and salt, and bring to a boil over high heat. Reduce the heat to low, cover the pan, and simmer for 20 minutes. With a slotted spoon, transfer the pieces of eel to an 8-by-12-by-2-inch baking dish, and stir the lemon juice into the cooking liquid. Discard the peppercorns. Then pour the entire contents of the pan over the eel, spreading the onion slices on top with a fork. Sprinkle evenly with the parsley, and refrigerate for at least 4 hours. When thoroughly chilled, the liquid should form a soft jelly.

Just before serving, arrange the slices of egg attractively on the jelly and serve directly from the bowl.

Kipper Paste

To make 2 cups

¼ pound butter plus 10 tablespoons
    butter cut into ½-inch bits and
    softened
2 pairs packaged smoked whole

Scottish kippers (about 2 pounds)
4 teaspoons anchovy paste
¼ teaspoon ground cloves
¼ teaspoon ground mace
⅛ teaspoon cayenne pepper

In a 1½- to 2-quart saucepan, clarify the ¼ pound of butter by melting it slow-ly over low heat. Skim off the surface foam and let the butter rest off the heat for a minute or two. Then spoon the clear butter on top into a bowl or cup, and discard the milky solids at the bottom of the pan.

Bring 1 quart of water to a boil in a heavy 10- to 12-inch skillet. Add the kip-pers, reduce the heat to low, and simmer uncovered for 5 minutes, or until the fish flakes easily when prodded with a fork. Drain the kippers and re-move the skin. With a fork, lift the meat away from the backbone and tail of each fish, but do not bother to remove the tiny bones. Discard the black roe.

Place the fish in the jar of an electric blender, and blend at high speed for 5 seconds. Add the anchovy paste, cloves, mace, cayenne pepper and 10 ta-blespoons of butter. Then continue to blend at high speed, stopping the motor occasionally to scrape down the sides of the jar with a rubber spatula, until the paste is smooth and creamy. (To make the paste by hand, mash the kippers as smoothly as possible with the back of a fork. Then beat in the bits of softened butter, a few pieces at a time, and finally the anchovy paste, cloves, mace and cayenne pepper.)

Spoon the kipper paste into a 2-cup serving dish at least 2½-inches deep, filling the bowl to within ¼ inch of the top. Seal by pouring the cooled clar-ified butter over the paste. Refrigerate for at least 6 hours, or until firm. Kip-per paste may be served on thinly sliced toast, or it may be used as a filling for sandwiches. Refrigerated and tightly covered, the paste can be kept for a week to 10 days.

Potted Shrimp

To serve 6

½ pound (2 sticks) plus 4 tablespoons butter, cut into ¼-inch bits
½ teaspoon mace
½ teaspoon ground nutmeg

⅛ teaspoon cayenne pepper
1 teaspoon salt
1 pound shelled, cooked tiny fresh shrimp (60 or more), or substitute 2 cups drained, canned tiny shrimp

In a 1½- to 2-quart saucepan, clarify ¼ pound of the butter by melting it slowly over low heat. Skim off the surface foam and let the butter rest off the heat for a minute or two. Then spoon the clear butter on top into a heavy 6- to 8-inch skillet and discard the milky solids at the bottom of the saucepan.

Melt the remaining ¼ pound plus 4 tablespoons of butter over moderate heat in a heavy 3- to 4-quart saucepan. When the foam begins to subside, stir in the mace, nutmeg, cayenne pepper and salt. Add the shrimp, turning them about with a spoon to coat them evenly.

Spoon the mixture into six 4-ounce individual baking dishes or custard cups, dividing the shrimp equally among them. Seal by pouring a thin layer of the clarified butter over each. Refrigerate the shrimp overnight or for at least 6 hours.

Potted shrimp are traditionally served with hot toast as a first course or at teatime.

Scotch Woodcock

SCRAMBLED EGGS ON ANCHOVY TOAST

To serve 4

4 eggs
3 tablespoons heavy cream
⅛ teaspoon salt
Freshly ground black pepper

3 tablespoons butter
4 slices hot buttered toast
2 tablespoons anchovy paste
8 flat anchovy fillets, thoroughly drained

In a small bowl, beat the eggs with a fork or whisk until they are well blended, then beat in the cream, salt and a few grindings of pepper. Place the skillet over low heat, and in it melt the 3 tablespoons of butter. Do not let the butter brown. Pour in the eggs and cook them over the lowest possible heat, stirring with the flat of a table fork or a rubber spatula, until they form soft, creamy curds. Do not overcook; the finished eggs should be moist. Quickly spread the toast with anchovy paste, arrange the slices on individual serving plates, and spread a layer of the scrambled eggs on top. Crisscross two anchovy fillets over each portion, and serve at once.

Meat, Poultry and Game

Roast Beef
To serve 6 to 8

An 8-pound standing 3-rib roast

Preheat the oven to 450° (it will take about 15 minutes for most ovens to reach this temperature). For the most predictable results, insert a meat thermometer into the thickest part of the beef, being careful not to let the tip of the thermometer touch any fat or bone.

Place the beef, fat side up, in a large shallow roasting pan. (It is unnecessary to use a rack, since the ribs of the roast form a natural rack.)

Roast the beef undisturbed in the middle of the oven for 20 minutes. Reduce the heat to 325° and continue to roast, without basting, for about 90 minutes, or until the beef is cooked to your taste. A meat thermometer will register 130° to 140° when the beef is rare, 150° to 160° when medium, and 160° to 170° when it is well done. If you are not using a thermometer, start timing the roast after you reduce the heat to 325°. You can estimate approximately 12 minutes per pound for rare beef, 15 minutes per pound for medium, and 20 minutes per pound for well done.

Transfer the beef to a heated platter and let it rest for at least 15 minutes for easier carving. If you plan to accompany the beef with Yorkshire pudding *(Recipe Index)*, increase the oven heat to 400° as soon as the beef is cooked. Transfer the roast from the oven to a heated platter, drape foil loosely over it, and set aside in a warm place while the pudding bakes. If you have two ovens, time the pudding to finish cooking during the 15 minutes that the roast rests.

To carve, first remove a thin slice of beef from the large end of the roast so that it will stand firmly on this end. Insert a large fork below the top rib and carve slices of beef from the top, separating each slice from the bone as you proceed. Traditionally, roast beef is served with its own juices and with a horseradish sauce *(Recipe Index)*.

NOTE: Bringing meat to room temperature before cooking it is unnecessary. Roasts may go directly from the refrigerator to the oven.

Boiled Beef and Carrots with Dumplings
To serve 6

MEAT

A 3- to 3½-pound lean corned beef
  brisket, rolled and tied

18 peeled white onions, about 1
  inch in diameter (about 1 pound)
12 small scraped carrots

Place the brisket in a 5- to 6-quart casserole, and add enough water to cover
it by at least ½ inch. Bring to a boil over high heat, meanwhile skimming
off the scum and foam as they rise to the surface. Reduce the heat, partially
cover the casserole, and simmer for 2½ hours. Then add the onions and carrots, and cook partially covered for another 30 minutes, or until the vegetables
are tender and the meat shows no resistance when pierced with a fork.

DUMPLINGS

1 cup all-purpose flour
½ teaspoon double-acting baking
  powder
½ teaspoon salt

1½ ounces fresh beef suet, finely
  chopped and thoroughly chilled
  (about 3 tablespoons)
⅓ cup milk

Meanwhile, preheat the oven to 250° and make the dumpling mixture.
Sift the flour, baking powder and salt into a large bowl. Add the suet and,
working quickly, rub the flour and fat together with your fingertips until
they look like flakes of coarse meal. Pour the milk over the mixture, toss together lightly, and gather the dough into a ball. If the dough crumbles, add
up to 2 more tablespoons of milk, a drop or two at a time, until the particles
adhere. With lightly floured hands, shape the dough into 1-inch balls.

With a slotted spoon, remove the meat and vegetables from the stock,
and arrange them on a large heated platter. Cover and keep them warm in
the oven. Drop the dumplings into the stock remaining in the casserole, stirring gently once or twice. Cook uncovered over moderate heat for 15 minutes,
or until the dumplings rise to the surface. Transfer the dumplings to the platter of beef and vegetables, and serve at once, accompanied if you like by
pease pudding (Recipe Index).

Deviled Beef Bones

SHORT RIBS IN A SPICY SAUCE

To serve 3 to 4

6 tablespoons butter, softened
1 tablespoon Worcestershire sauce
1 teaspoon dry English mustard
1 teaspoon curry powder (preferably imported Madras curry powder)

Freshly ground black pepper
1/4 teaspoon cayenne pepper
1 teaspoon salt
2 1/2 to 3 pounds lean short ribs of beef, each 4 to 5 inches long
1/2 cup flour

Preheat the oven to 450°. With a pastry brush and 2 tablespoons of the softened butter, coat the bottom and sides of a shallow roasting pan large enough to hold the short ribs in one layer. In a small bowl, cream the remaining 4 tablespoons of softened butter by beating and mashing it against the sides of the bowl with a large spoon until it is light and fluffy. Then beat in the Worcestershire sauce, mustard, curry powder, 1 teaspoon of black pepper, cayenne pepper and 1/2 teaspoon of the salt. Set aside.

With a small, sharp knife, make 1/4-inch-deep crisscrossing cuts about 1 inch apart on the meaty surface of the ribs. Then coat them with the flour and shake them vigorously to remove any excess. Sprinkle the ribs with the remaining 1/2 teaspoon of salt and a few grindings of pepper and arrange them fat side up in a single layer in the roasting pan. Roast in the middle of the oven for 10 minutes. Using a pastry brush coat the ribs evenly with the seasoned butter, reduce the heat to 400°, and roast for 1 hour and 15 minutes, or until the meat is tender and shows no resistance when pierced with the tip of a fork. Arrange the ribs on a large platter and serve at once.

NOTE: Traditionally, the bones deviled were those left over from a standing rib roast. They were simply spread with the seasoned butter and broiled until brown and crusty.

Oxtail Stew

To serve 6

3½ to 4 pounds oxtail, cut into 2-inch lengths
1½ teaspoons salt
Freshly ground black pepper
1 cup flour
6 tablespoons rendered bacon fat or lard
1 medium-sized carrot, scraped and coarsely chopped
1 medium-sized turnip, scraped and coarsely chopped
1 small celery stalk, coarsely chopped
1 large onion, coarsely chopped
3 cups beef stock, fresh or canned
1 small bay leaf
¼ teaspoon thyme
3 sprigs fresh parsley

Preheat the oven to 325°. Wipe the pieces of oxtail with a dampened towel, then sprinkle them with salt and a few grindings of pepper. Dip the pieces in flour and shake them vigorously to remove any excess. In a heavy 12-inch skillet, melt the fat or lard over high heat until it splutters. Add the oxtail (in two batches if necessary) and cook, turning frequently, until the pieces are brown on all sides, regulating the heat so that they color quickly and evenly without burning. With tongs, transfer the meat to a heavy 5- to 6-quart casserole or Dutch oven.

Add the carrot, turnip, celery and onion to the fat remaining in the skillet, and cook over moderate heat, stirring frequently, for 8 to 10 minutes, or until the vegetables are soft and light brown. Spread the vegetables over the oxtail. Then pour in the stock and add the bay leaf, thyme and parsley. Bring to a boil over high heat, cover, and bake in the middle of the oven for 2½ hours, or until the meat can easily be pulled away from the bone with a fork. With a large spoon, skim as much fat from the surface of the cooking juices as you can. Taste for seasoning and serve directly from the casserole.

Beef Roll

To serve 4 to 6

1 pound lean boneless top round, chuck or shin of beef, coarsely ground
½ pound lean boneless uncooked ham, coarsely ground
1 cup fresh soft crumbs, made from homemade-type white bread, pulverized in a blender or shredded with a fork
¼ teaspoon ground nutmeg
1½ teaspoons salt
¼ teaspoon freshly ground pepper
1 egg, lightly beaten

In a large bowl, combine the beef, ham, crumbs, nutmeg, salt and pepper. Add the egg and beat vigorously with a spoon until the ingredients are well blended. Do not overbeat; the texture should be somewhat coarse. Spoon the meat mixture into a 4- to 6-cup pudding mold, or any other plain mold, packing it down firmly. Cover the mold with its lid or a sheet of buttered foil.

Place the mold in a deep pot and pour in enough cold water to come halfway up the sides of the mold. Bring to a boil over high heat, reduce the heat to low, cover the pot tightly, and simmer for 2 hours. Replenish the water in the pot with more boiling water when necessary.

Remove the mold from the pot, remove the cover or foil, and cover the beef roll with fresh foil. Place a plate over the top of the mold, and weight it with a heavy pan or casserole weighing about 3 or 4 pounds. Cool to room temperature, then refrigerate, with the weight still in place, for 4 to 5 hours, or until the roll is thoroughly chilled. Unmold the beef roll in the following fashion: Run a sharp knife around the sides of the mold, and dip the bottom in hot water for a few seconds. Wipe the outside of the mold dry, place an inverted serving plate over the mold and, grasping both plate and mold together firmly, turn them over. Rap the plate on a table and the beef roll should slide out easily. Traditionally, beef roll is served with mustard and accompanied by freshly baked bread and butter.

Spiced Beef

To serve 8 to 12

¼ cup dark-brown sugar
A 3- to 4-pound lean fresh brisket of beef
¼ cup whole juniper berries
1 tablespoon whole allspice
1 tablespoon whole black peppercorns
¼ cup coarse (kosher) salt
¾ cup cold water

NOTE: This old traditional recipe is a comparatively simple one, but the beef does require almost 2 weeks of marination.

With your fingertips, firmly press the brown sugar into the brisket. When the meat is well coated on all sides, place it in a 5- to 6-quart casserole or baking dish. Cover and refrigerate undisturbed for 2 days.

With a mortar and pestle, crush the juniper berries, allspice, peppercorns and salt together, or wrap them in a towel and crush with a rolling pin. Once a day for 9 days, press about 1 tablespoon of the spice mixture into the surface of the meat, cover and return it to the refrigerator.

On the 12th day, preheat the oven to 275°. Rinse the beef under cold running water to remove any spices adhering to it, and pour off all the accumulated liquid in the casserole. Return the beef to the casserole and add the ¾ cup of water. Cover and bake undisturbed in the middle of the oven for 3½ hours, or until the meat is tender and shows no resistance when pierced with a fork. Then cool the meat to room temperature and wrap it in foil. Place a flat plate or board on top of it, and weight it with a heavy pan or casserole weighing at least 3 or 4 pounds. Refrigerate the weighted meat overnight or for at least 12 hours. To serve, carve the beef into the thinnest possible slices and accompany it with freshly baked bread and butter.

Tightly wrapped in foil and refrigerated, spiced beef will keep for as long as 4 weeks. When the beef is fully chilled, the weight may be removed.

Scotch Broth
To serve 6 to 8

2 pounds lamb neck or shoulder with bones, cut into 6 pieces	½ cup finely chopped carrots
2 quarts cold water	½ cup finely chopped turnips
2 tablespoons barley	½ cup finely chopped onions
2 teaspoons salt	½ cup finely chopped leeks, including 2 inches of green
⅛ teaspoon freshly ground black pepper	½ cup finely chopped celery
	1 tablespoon finely chopped parsley

Place the lamb in a heavy 4- to 5-quart casserole and add the water. Bring to a boil over high heat, meanwhile skimming off the foam and scum as they rise to the surface. Add the barley, salt and pepper, reduce the heat to low, and simmer partially covered for 1 hour. Add the carrots, turnips, onions, leeks and celery, partially cover again, and cook for 1 hour more. With a slotted spoon, transfer the lamb to a plate and pull or cut the meat away from the bones. Discard the bones, fat and gristle, and cut the meat into ½-inch cubes. Return the meat to the soup and simmer for 2 or 3 minutes to heat it through. Taste for seasoning. Sprinkle with parsley before serving.

Roast Leg of Lamb with Mint Sauce

To serve 6 to 8

MINT SAUCE
1/4 cup water
1 tablespoon sugar

1/4 cup finely chopped fresh mint
leaves
1/2 cup malt vinegar

Make the mint sauce in advance. Combine the water and sugar in a 1- to 1½-quart saucepan, and bring to a boil over high heat, stirring until the sugar dissolves completely.

Remove the pan from the heat, and stir in the mint leaves and vinegar. Taste and add up to 1 more tablespoon of sugar if desired. Set aside at room temperature for 2 or 3 hours.

MEAT
2 tablespoons salt
1 teaspoon finely ground black
  pepper
1 tablespoon finely cut fresh
  rosemary or 2 teaspoons dried

crushed rosemary
A 5- to 6-pound leg of lamb,
  trimmed of excess fat, but with
  the fell (the parchmentlike
  covering) left on

Preheat the oven to 500° (it will take about 15 minutes for most ovens to reach this temperature). Combine the salt, pepper and rosemary in a small bowl, and with your fingers press the mixture firmly into the lamb, coating the entire surface as evenly as possible. For the most predictable results, insert a meat thermometer into the thickest part of the leg, being careful not to touch a bone.

Place the leg, fat side up, on a rack in a shallow roasting pan, and roast it uncovered in the middle of the oven for 20 minutes. Reduce the heat to 375° and roast for another 40 to 60 minutes, or until the lamb is cooked to your taste (basting is unnecessary). A meat thermometer will register 130° to 140° when the lamb is rare, 140° to 150° when medium, and 150° to 160° when well done.

Transfer the lamb to a heated platter, and let the roast rest for 15 minutes for easier carving. Stir the mint sauce once or twice, pour it into a sauceboat and serve it separately with the lamb.

Lancashire Hot Pot

LAMB-CHOP CASSEROLE WITH KIDNEYS AND OYSTERS

To serve 6

1 tablespoon butter, softened, plus
   1 tablespoon butter, cut into ¼-
   inch bits
6 medium-sized potatoes, peeled and
   cut crosswise into ¼-inch slices
6 lean shoulder lamb chops (about
   2 pounds), each cut about 1 inch
   thick and trimmed of all fat
1 teaspoon salt
Freshly ground black pepper
6 lamb kidneys, membranes

removed, trimmed of all fat, and
   cut crosswise into ¼-inch slices
6 shucked oysters (optional)
½ pound fresh mushrooms,
   including stems, cut lengthwise
   into ¼-inch slices
3 medium-sized onions (about 1
   pound), peeled and cut crosswise
   into ⅛-inch slices
2 cups water
1 tablespoon finely chopped parsley

Preheat the oven to 350°. Using a pastry brush, coat the bottom and sides of a 4- to 5-quart casserole at least 6 inches deep with the 1 tablespoon of softened butter. Spread about one third of the potato slices evenly over the bottom of the casserole, and place 3 lamb chops side by side on top. Sprinkle the chops with ½ teaspoon of the salt and a few grindings of pepper. Add half the kidneys, 3 oysters, half the mushrooms and half the onions, and cover with another third of the potatoes. Place the 3 remaining chops on the potatoes and sprinkle them with the remaining salt and a few grindings of pepper. Add the remaining kidneys, oysters, mushrooms and onions, and spread the rest of the potatoes evenly over the top. Pour in the water. Dot with the bits of butter. Cover and bake in the middle of the oven for 1½ hours. Remove the cover and bake for 30 minutes longer, or until the top is brown. Sprinkle with parsley and serve directly from the casserole.

Irish Stew
To serve 4 to 6

6 medium-sized peeled potatoes (about 2 pounds), cut crosswise into ¼-inch slices
4 large onions (about 1½ pounds), peeled and cut into ¼-inch slices
3 pounds lean boneless lamb neck or shoulder, trimmed of all fat and cut into 1-inch cubes
1 teaspoon salt
Freshly ground black pepper
¼ teaspoon thyme
Cold water

Spread half the potatoes on the bottom of a heavy 4- to 5-quart casserole or Dutch oven, and cover them with half the onion slices and then all the lamb. Sprinkle with ½ teaspoon of the salt, a few grindings of pepper and the thyme. Arrange the rest of the onions over the meat and spread the remaining potatoes on top. Sprinkle with ½ teaspoon of salt and a few grindings of pepper, then pour in enough cold water just to cover the potatoes.

Bring the stew to a boil over high heat, reduce the heat to its lowest possible point, and cover the casserole tightly. Simmer for 1½ hours. Check from time to time and add boiling water, a tablespoon or two at a time, if the liquid seems to be cooking away.

Serve the stew directly from the casserole or Dutch oven, ladling it into heated deep individual serving plates. Traditionally, Irish stew is accompanied by pickled red cabbage (Recipe Index).

NOTE: If you prefer, you may cook the stew in a preheated 350° oven instead of on top of the stove. In that event, bring the casserole to a boil on top of the stove before placing it in the lower third of the oven.

Deviled Kidneys
To serve 4

8 whole lamb kidneys, peeled and trimmed of fat
2 teaspoons bottled mango chutney, finely chopped
1 tablespoon prepared mustard
1½ teaspoons dry English mustard
2 teaspoons fresh lemon juice
½ teaspoon salt
Pinch of cayenne pepper
1 tablespoon butter, softened
4 slices hot buttered toast

With a large, sharp knife, split the kidneys in half lengthwise without cutting all the way through. For the marinade, combine the chutney, prepared mustard, dry mustard, lemon juice, salt and cayenne pepper in a large mixing bowl, and stir until thoroughly mixed.

Add the kidneys and turn them about with a spoon to coat them evenly on all sides. Set the kidneys aside at room temperature to marinate for 1 hour, stirring them from time to time.

Remove the broiler pan from the oven and, using a pastry brush, coat it with softened butter. Setting the pan aside, preheat the broiler to its highest point. Then remove the kidneys from the marinade and spread them out flat on the pan, cut side up. Broil the kidneys 3 inches from the heat for 3 minutes. Turn them over with tongs and broil them 3 minutes more. Spread about ½ teaspoon of the marinade on each slice of toast, arrange the kidneys in pairs on the toast, and serve at once.

Toad-in-the-Hole
SAUSAGES BAKED IN BATTER

To serve 4

1 cup all-purpose flour	½ teaspoon salt
2 eggs	Freshly ground black pepper
1 cup milk	1 pound small, fresh pork sausages

To make the batter in a blender, combine the flour, eggs, milk, salt and a few grindings of pepper in the blender jar, and blend at high speed for 2 or 3 seconds. Turn off the machine, scrape down the sides of the jar, and blend again for 40 seconds. (To make the batter by hand, beat the eggs and salt with a whisk or a rotary or electric beater until frothy. Slowly add the flour, beating constantly. Then pour in the milk in a thin stream and beat until the mixture is smooth and creamy.) Refrigerate the batter for at least 1 hour.

Preheat the oven to 400°. Place the sausages side by side in a heavy 10- to 12-inch skillet, and prick them once or twice with the tines of a fork. Sprinkle them with 2 tablespoons of water, cover the pan tightly, and cook over low heat for 3 minutes. Then remove the cover, increase the heat to moderate, and continue to cook, turning the sausages frequently with tongs or a spatula, until the water has completely evaporated and the sausages have begun to brown in their own fat.

Arrange the sausages in a single layer in a baking tin or dish about 6 by 10 inches and 2 inches deep, and moisten them with 2 tablespoons of their drippings. Keep them at least an inch apart. Then pour the batter over them and bake in the middle of the oven for 30 minutes, or until the pudding has risen over the top of the pan and is crisp and brown. Serve at once.

Potted Pork

To make about 1½ cups

¾ pound lean boneless pork, cut
  into ½-inch cubes
¼ pound fresh pork fat, cut into ¼-
  inch cubes
½ teaspoon salt
Freshly ground black pepper
½ cup water
1 large bay leaf
2 whole cloves

Preheat the oven to 275°. In a heavy 2- to 3-quart casserole, toss together the pork, pork fat, salt and a few grindings of pepper. Pour in the water, add the bay leaf and cloves, and cover tightly. Bake in the middle of the oven for 4 hours, or until most of the liquid has evaporated and the pork is tender enough to be mashed against the side of the casserole with a spoon. Do not let the pork brown. Check the casserole occasionally and, if the liquid seems to be cooking away, add more water a tablespoon or so at a time.

With a slotted spoon, transfer the pork to a shallow bowl. Discard the bay leaf and cloves, and reserve all the fat and cooking juices. Cut away any bits of gristle and shred the pork as fine as possible with a fork. Stir in the reserved fat and juices, then pack the mixture tightly into a 2-cup mold, a terrine or an earthenware crock. Cover with a lid or foil, and refrigerate for at least 24 hours before serving. Potted pork is traditionally served with hot toast as a first course or at teatime.

Brawn

JELLED PIGS' FEET AND BEEF

To serve 4 to 6

6 fresh pigs' feet (about 3½ to 4
  pounds)
1 pound boneless beef shin
1 tablespoon salt plus 1½ teaspoons
  salt
1 cup coarsely chopped onions
4 whole cloves, coarsely crushed with
  a mortar and pestle or wrapped
  in a towel and crushed with a
  rolling pin
Freshly ground black pepper

Wash the pigs' feet thoroughly under cold running water, then place them with the beef in an 8- to 10-quart pot. Pour in enough cold water to cover the meats by about 1 inch. Add 1 tablespoon of salt, and bring to a boil over high heat, meanwhile skimming off the scum and foam that rise to the surface. Then add the chopped onions and cloves, and reduce the heat to low. Simmer partially covered for about 2 hours, until the meats are tender and show no resistance when pierced with the tines of a fork. Transfer the meats to a platter and strain the cooking liquid through a fine sieve set over a bowl.

While the pigs' feet are still hot, remove their skin and bones, and discard them. Coarsely chop the meat from the feet and the beef shin and place it in a mixing bowl. Add 1 cup of the strained cooking liquid, 1½ teaspoons of salt and a few grindings of pepper, and mix thoroughly. Then pour the entire contents of the bowl into a 1-pint loaf pan or mold. Cover the top with wax paper or foil and weight it with a heavy pan or casserole weighing 3 or 4 pounds. Cool to room temperature, then refrigerate the brawn, with the weight still in place, for at least 6 hours or until it jellies.

To unmold and serve the brawn, run a sharp knife around the side of the pan and dip the bottom in hot water for a few seconds. Wipe the pan dry, place a chilled serving plate over it and, grasping pan and plate firmly together, quickly turn them over. Rap them sharply on a table and the brawn should slide out easily. Cut the brawn into ¼-inch crosswise slices and arrange the slices attractively on a chilled serving plate, overlapping them slightly. Brawn may be served as a first course or as a light luncheon dish. Accompany it with fresh bread and pickled onions (*Recipe Index*).

Cockaleekie
CHICKEN-AND-LEEK SOUP

To make 4 to 5 quarts soup	to remove any hidden pockets of sand, and cut diagonally into ½-inch slices (about 8 cups)
A 5½- to 6-pound stewing fowl	½ cup barley
5 quarts cold water	1 tablespoon salt
10 large leeks, including 2 inches of the green stems, thoroughly washed	2 tablespoons finely chopped parsley

Wash the fowl thoroughly inside and out under cold running water. Remove and discard any chunks of fat from the cavity, and place the bird in a 10- to 12-quart soup pot. Pour in the 5 quarts of water and bring to a boil over high heat, meanwhile skimming off the foam and scum that will rise to the surface. Add the leeks, barley and salt, and reduce the heat to low.

Partially cover the pot and simmer for 3 to 3½ hours, or until the bird is almost falling apart. Then transfer it to a platter and, with a large spoon, skim almost all of the fat from the surface of the soup.

When the fowl is cool enough to handle, remove the skin and pull the meat from the bones with your fingers or a small knife. Discard the skin and bones and cut the meat into thin shreds about 2 inches long. Return the meat to the soup. Simmer for 2 or 3 minutes to heat the meat through and then taste the soup for seasoning.

To serve, pour the soup into a heated tureen or ladle it into individual soup plates, and sprinkle with chopped parsley.

Hindle Wakes

COLD STUFFED CHICKEN WITH LEMON-AND-CREAM SAUCE

To serve 6 to 8

STUFFING

2 cups (1 pound) coarsely chopped
   pitted dried prunes
4 cups coarsely crumbled day-old
   homemade-type white bread

½ cup finely chopped beef suet
¼ teaspoon dried marjoram
1 teaspoon salt
½ teaspoon freshly ground black
   pepper
½ cup malt vinegar

To make the stuffing, combine the 2 cups of prunes, the crumbs, suet, marjoram, 1 teaspoon of salt and black pepper, and toss them about in a bowl with a spoon until well blended. Then stir in the ½ cup of vinegar.

CHICKEN

A 5- to 6-pound roasting chicken
1 teaspoon plus 2 tablespoons salt
1 stalk celery, cut into 2-inch lengths
1 large onion, studded with 4 whole
   cloves

1 large bay leaf
4 parsley sprigs
3 quarts water
1 cup malt vinegar
1 tablespoon dark-brown sugar

Wash the chicken under cold running water and pat it completely dry inside and out with paper towels. Sprinkle the cavity with 1 teaspoon of the salt and loosely spoon in the stuffing. Close the opening by lacing it with skewers or by sewing it with heavy white thread. Fasten the neck skin to the back of the chicken with a skewer and truss the bird securely.

Place the chicken in a heavy 6- to 8-quart casserole and arrange the celery stalk, onion, bay leaf and parsley around it. Pour in the water and 1 cup of vinegar, and add the remaining 2 tablespoons of salt and the brown sugar. The water should rise at least 2 inches above the chicken; add more if necessary. Bring to a boil over high heat, skimming off the scum and foam as they rise to the surface. Reduce the heat to low, partially cover the pot, and simmer for 1½ to 2 hours, or until the chicken is tender but not falling apart.

Let the chicken cool in its stock to room temperature. Then place it on a large platter and discard the stock.

SAUCE

½ cup heavy cream

A pinch of white pepper

4 tablespoons fresh lemon juice

1 tablespoon butter

2 teaspoons finely grated lemon peel

1 tablespoon flour

⅛ teaspoon ground thyme

½ cup milk

In a 1- to 1½-quart enameled or stainless-steel saucepan, bring the cream, lemon juice, 1 teaspoon of the grated lemon peel, the thyme and a pinch of white pepper to a simmer over low heat. Simmer for 2 or 3 minutes, then strain the cream through a fine sieve set over a bowl. Set aside.

In a heavy 8- to 10-inch skillet, melt the butter over moderate heat. When the foam begins to subside, stir in the flour and mix thoroughly. Pour in the milk and, stirring constantly with a whisk, cook over high heat until the mixture thickens slightly and comes to a boil. Reduce the heat to low and simmer for about 3 minutes to remove any taste of raw flour. Then stir in the strained cream and simmer just long enough to heat the sauce through. Taste for seasoning and cool the sauce to room temperature.

GARNISH

Lemon quarters or slices

halves

6 pitted prunes, cut lengthwise into

Parsley sprigs

To assemble the hindle wakes, pour the sauce over the top of the bird and sprinkle it with 1 teaspoon of grated lemon peel. Arrange the lemons, prune halves and parsley sprigs attractively around the chicken, and serve at room temperature.

Rabbit Stew

To serve 6 to 8

⅓ cup dry red wine
2 tablespoons olive oil
1 large onion, cut into ⅛-inch-thick
slices
3 whole juniper berries, wrapped in
a kitchen towel and crushed with
a rolling pin or crushed with a
mortar and pestle
1 large bay leaf
½ teaspoon crumbled dried rosemary
1½ teaspoons salt
Freshly ground black pepper
A 5- to 6-pound fresh rabbit or
defrosted frozen rabbit, cut into 2-
inch-square pieces, or substitute
two 2½- to 3-pound fresh or

defrosted frozen rabbits, cut in 2-
inch-square pieces
2 tablespoons flour
6 slices lean bacon, coarsely chopped
¼ cup finely chopped shallots, or
substitute ¼ cup chopped onions
½ cup coarsely chopped celery
6 small carrots, scraped and coarsely
chopped
1½ cups chicken stock, fresh or
canned
1 teaspoon dried thyme
2 teaspoons finely chopped parsley
2 small bay leaves
½ cup port
3 tablespoons red currant jelly *(page 4)*

Combine the wine, olive oil, sliced onion, juniper berries, bay leaf, rosemary, ½ teaspoon of the salt and a few grindings of black pepper in a large bowl. Wash the rabbit under cold running water, pat it thoroughly dry with paper towels and place it in the bowl. Turn the pieces about with a spoon until they are thoroughly coated with the marinade, cover the bowl and marinate the rabbit for at least 6 hours at room temperature, or 12 hours in the refrigerator. In either case, turn the pieces about in the marinade occasionally to keep them well moistened.

Drain the rabbit in a colander set over a bowl. Reserve the liquid, but discard the onion and herbs. Pat the pieces of rabbit completely dry with paper towels, then coat them with the flour, shaking each piece vigorously to remove the excess.

In a heavy 4- to 5-quart flameproof casserole, cook the bacon over moderate heat, stirring occasionally, until crisp and brown. With a slotted spoon, transfer the bacon to paper towels to drain. Add the rabbit to the fat remaining in the casserole and brown it, turning the pieces with tongs and regulating the heat so that the rabbit colors quickly and evenly on all sides without burning. Transfer the browned rabbit from the casserole to a plate.

Pour off all but 2 tablespoons of fat from the casserole, add the shallots, celery and carrots, and cook for 5 minutes, or until the vegetables are soft but not brown. Pour in the reserved marinade and the chicken stock and bring to a boil over high heat, meanwhile scraping in any brown particles clinging to the bottom and sides of the casserole. Add the thyme, parsley, bay leaves, teaspoon of salt and a few grindings of pepper, and return the rabbit and the bacon to the casserole.

Cover tightly and bake in the middle of the oven for 1 hour. Stir in the port and currant jelly, cover again, and bake for 30 minutes longer, or until the rabbit is tender but not falling apart. (If you are substituting small rabbits, they may cook much faster. Watch carefully that they do not overcook.) Taste for seasoning.

Serve the rabbit directly from the casserole. It may be accompanied by forcemeat balls *(below)*.

Forcemeat Balls

To make about 12 balls

⅛ pound fresh beef suet, finely chopped
¼ cup finely chopped cooked smoked ham (about ⅛ pound)
2 cups fresh soft crumbs, made from homemade-type white bread, pulverized in a blender or shredded with a fork

2 teaspoons finely chopped parsley
1 teaspoon finely grated lemon peel
¼ teaspoon ground thyme
¼ teaspoon ground sage
½ teaspoon salt
Freshly ground black pepper
1 egg, lightly beaten
2 tablespoons butter
2 tablespoons vegetable oil

In a large bowl, combine the suet, ham, bread crumbs, parsley, lemon peel, thyme, sage, salt and a few grindings of pepper. Stir thoroughly, then add the egg and mix together until the forcemeat can be gathered into a ball. Divide it into 12 equal pieces and, with lightly moistened hands, shape each piece into a ball about 1½ inches in diameter.

In a heavy 10- to 12-inch skillet, melt the butter in the oil over moderate heat. When the foam has almost subsided, drop in the balls. Cook them for about 5 minutes, or until golden brown on all sides, turning them frequently with a spoon and regulating the heat so that they color slowly and evenly without burning. With a slotted spoon, transfer the balls to a double thickness of paper towels to drain briefly, and serve.

NOTE: Forcemeat balls traditionally accompany game dishes like rabbit stew *(above)*.

Roast Pheasant
To serve 4 to 6

A 3½- to 4-pound oven-ready
   pheasant
½ teaspoon salt
Freshly ground black pepper

4 ounces ground beef
2 tablespoons butter, softened, plus
   ½ cup butter, melted
4 slices lean bacon

Preheat the oven to 350°. Wash the pheasant quickly under cold running water and pat it thoroughly dry inside and out with paper towels. Rub the inside of the bird with the salt and a few grindings of pepper and place the ground beef in the cavity. Close the opening by lacing it with skewers or sewing it with heavy white thread.

Fasten the neck skin to the back of the pheasant with a skewer, and, using a pastry brush, coat the skin of the bird evenly with the 2 tablespoons of softened butter. Drape the bacon slices side by side over the breast and wrap them around the bird, pressing the slices snugly against the body to keep them in place.

Place the pheasant, breast side up, on a rack in a shallow roasting pan just large enough to hold the bird comfortably. Roast undisturbed in the middle of the oven for 20 minutes, then increase the oven heat to 400°. Remove and discard the bacon slices. Using a pastry brush, baste the pheasant with 2 tablespoons of melted butter and roast it for about 20 minutes longer, basting generously every 5 minutes or so with a few tablespoons of the remaining melted butter.

To test whether the bird is done, pierce the thigh with the tip of a small, sharp knife. The juice should spurt out a clear yellow; if it is still pink, roast the pheasant for another 5 to 10 minutes.

Transfer the pheasant to a heated platter and let it rest for 10 minutes for easier carving. Discard the ground beef, which is used to keep the bird moist during the cooking and is not intended as a stuffing.

The roast pheasant is traditionally served with bread sauce *(Recipe Index)* and game chips *(Recipe Index)*, and may be decorated with bunches of watercress and its own tail feathers before serving.

Savory Puddings and Pies

Suet Pastry

½ pound finely chopped beef suet,   1 teaspoon salt
   thoroughly chilled   Freshly ground black pepper
4 cups all-purpose flour   6 to 8 tablespoons ice water

In a large chilled mixing bowl, combine the suet, flour, salt and a few grindings of pepper. With your fingertips rub the flour and fat together until they look like flakes of coarse meal. Pour 6 tablespoons of ice water over the mixture all at once, knead together vigorously and gather the dough into a ball. If the dough crumbles, add up to 2 more tablespoons of ice water, 1 teaspoon at a time, until the particles adhere.

Gather the dough into a ball and place it on a lightly floured surface. Knead, pressing the dough flat, pushing it forward and folding it back on itself for 6 to 8 minutes, or until it is smooth and satiny. Dust the suet pastry with a little flour and wrap it in wax paper. Refrigerate at least 1 hour before using.

Hot-Water Pastry

5 cups all-purpose flour
½ teaspoon salt   6 tablespoons milk
10 tablespoons lard   2 tablespoons water

In a deep bowl, combine the flour and salt. Warm the lard, milk and water in a saucepan over moderate heat, and stir until the lard melts. Beat the mixture, a few tablespoons at a time, into the flour, and continue to beat until the dough can be gathered into a compact ball. On a lightly floured surface, knead the dough for 2 or 3 minutes by pressing it down, pushing it forward, and folding it back on itself until it is smooth and elastic. Again gather it into a ball. Place it in a bowl and drape a dampened kitchen towel over it. Let the dough rest for 30 minutes before using.

NOTE: This pastry is traditionally used for veal-and-ham pie *(Recipe Index)* and pork pie.

Yorkshire Pudding

To serve 6 to 8

2 eggs	1 cup milk
½ teaspoon salt	2 tablespoons roast beef drippings,
1 cup all-purpose flour	or substitute 2 tablespoons lard

To make the batter in a blender, combine the eggs, salt, flour and milk in the blender jar, and blend at high speed for 2 or 3 seconds. Turn off the machine, scrape down the sides of the jar, and blend again for 40 seconds. (To make the batter by hand, beat the eggs and salt with a whisk or a rotary or electric beater until frothy. Slowly add the flour, beating constantly. Then pour in the milk in a thin stream and beat until the mixture is smooth and creamy.) Refrigerate for at least 1 hour.

Preheat the oven to 400°. In a 10-by-15-by-2½-inch roasting pan, heat the fat over moderate heat until it splutters. Briefly beat the batter again and pour it into the pan. Bake in the middle of the oven for 15 minutes, reduce the heat to 375°, and bake for 15 minutes longer, or until the pudding has risen over the top of the pan and is crisp and brown. With a sharp knife, divide the pudding into portions, and serve immediately.

Yorkshire pudding is always served with roast beef *(Recipe Index)*. The same batter is used to make toad-in-the-hole *(Recipe Index)*.

Veal-and-Ham Pie

To serve 6 to 8

2 tablespoons butter, softened	1 teaspoon crumbled dried sage leaves
2 pounds lean boneless veal, cut into ¼-inch cubes	2 teaspoons salt
1 pound lean smoked ham, cut into ¼-inch cubes	¼ teaspoon freshly ground black pepper
¼ cup finely chopped parsley	Hot-water pastry *(page 63)*
6 tablespoons brandy	4 hard-cooked eggs
6 tablespoons fresh or canned chicken or beef stock	8 to 10 pickled walnuts (optional)
2 tablespoons fresh lemon juice	1 egg yolk combined with 1 tablespoon heavy cream
1 teaspoon finely grated lemon peel	1 envelope unflavored gelatin
	2 cups chicken stock, fresh or canned

Preheat the oven to 350°. Using a pastry brush, coat the bottom and sides of a 10-by-5-by-4-inch loaf mold with the butter. Set aside. In a large bowl, combine the veal, ham, parsley, brandy, stock, lemon juice, peel, sage, salt and pepper. Toss the ingredients about with a spoon until thoroughly mixed.

Break off about one third of the hot-water pastry and set it aside. On a lightly floured surface, roll out the remaining pastry into a rectangle about 20 inches long, 10 inches wide and ¼ inch thick. Drape the pastry over the rolling pin, lift it up, and unroll it slackly over the mold. Gently press the pastry into the mold. Roll the pin over the rim to trim off the excess pastry.

Spoon enough of the veal and ham mixture into the pastry shell to fill it a little less than half full. Arrange the hard-cooked eggs in a single row down the center of the mold, and line up the pickled walnuts, if you are using them, on both sides of the eggs. Cover the eggs with the remaining meat mixture, filling the shell to within 1 inch of the top.

Roll the reserved pastry into a 4-by-13-inch rectangle ¼ inch thick. Lift it up on the pin and drape it over the top of the mold. Trim off the excess with a small knife and, with the tines of a fork or your fingers, crimp the pastry to secure it to the rim of the mold. Then cut a 1-inch round hole in the center of the pie. Roll out the scraps of pastry and cut them into leaf and flower shapes. Moisten their bottom sides with the egg-and-cream mixture and arrange on the pie. Brush the entire surface with the egg-and-cream mixture.

Bake the pie in the middle of the oven for 2 hours, or until the top is a deep golden brown. Remove from the oven and cool for 15 minutes.

Meanwhile, in a 1- to 1½-quart saucepan, sprinkle the gelatin over 2 cups of cold chicken stock and let it soften for 2 or 3 minutes. Then set the pan over low heat and cook, stirring constantly, until the gelatin dissolves completely. Pour the gelatin through a funnel into the opening of the pie. Cool the pie to room temperature, then refrigerate it for at least 6 hours, or until the aspic is set. Ideally the pie should be removed from the refrigerator about 30 minutes before being served.

To unmold and serve the pie, run the blade of a sharp knife around the inside edges of the mold and dip the bottom of the mold in hot water. Wipe the mold dry, place an inverted serving plate over it and, grasping mold and plate together firmly, quickly turn them over. Rap the plate on a table and the pie should slide out easily. Turn the pie over and serve, cut into ½-inch-thick slices.

NOTE: Traditionally, veal-and-ham pies are "raised pies." That is, the pastry casing for the pie is "raised," or shaped, around a wooden mold.

Steak-and-Kidney Pudding

To serve 4 to 6

2 pounds lean boneless beef chuck
  or top round, cut into 1-inch cubes
1 pound veal or lamb kidneys, peeled
  and trimmed of fat, and cut into
  1-inch cubes
2/3 cup flour
1/4 teaspoon ground nutmeg
1 1/2 teaspoons salt

1/4 teaspoon freshly ground black
  pepper
1/4 pound large fresh mushrooms,
  trimmed and cut into quarters,
  including the stems
1/2 cup coarsely chopped onions
1/4 cup finely chopped parsley
Suet pastry *(page 63)*
1 1/2 cups boiling water

Place the cubes of beef and kidney in a large mixing bowl. Combine 1/3 cup of the flour with the nutmeg, salt and pepper, and sift it over the meat. Then toss together with a large spoon to coat the pieces evenly. Stir in the mushrooms, onions and parsley. Set aside.

On a lightly floured surface, roll out about two thirds of the suet pastry into a rough circle 14 inches in diameter and 1/4 inch thick. Drape the pastry over the rolling pin and unfold it slackly over a 6-cup English pudding basin or a plain 6-cup mold about 7 inches in diameter and 4 inches deep. Gently press the pastry into the basin, being careful not to stretch it. Roll out the remaining pastry into an 8-inch circle, and set it aside.

Ladle the beef-and-kidney mixture into the mold, filling it to within 1/2 inch of the top. Mound the meat in the center, and pour in the water.

With a sharp knife, trim the excess pastry from the rim of the mold and lightly moisten the rim with a pastry brush dipped in cold water. Carefully place the 8-inch circle of pastry over the mold and trim the edges again. Then crimp the pastry all around the rim with your fingers or the tines of a fork to seal it tightly. Lay a lightly buttered 10-inch circle of parchment paper or foil over the top of the pudding, turning the edges down all around its circumference to hold it in place.

Now dampen a cloth kitchen towel with cold water and wring it dry. Spread the towel flat, sprinkle it evenly with the remaining 1/3 cup of flour, and shake it vigorously to dislodge the excess flour. Spread the towel, floured side down, over the top of the pudding. Bring the ends of the towel down around the sides of the basin or mold and tie them in place about 1 1/2 to 2 inches down the side (just below the rim if you are using a pudding basin) with a long length of kitchen cord. Bring up two diagonally opposite corners of the towel and tie them together on top of the pudding. Then bring the remaining corners together and tie them similarly.

Place the pudding in a large pot and pour in enough boiling water to come three fourths of the way up the side of the mold. Bring to a boil, cover the pot tightly, reduce the heat to its lowest point, and steam for 5 hours. From time to time replenish the water in the pot with additional boiling water.

To serve, lift the pudding out of the water (holding it by the looped cloth if you are using a basin with a rim) and remove the towel and paper or foil. Wipe the mold completely dry and wrap it in a clean linen napkin. Serve at the table directly from the basin or mold.

Pork-and-Apple Pie

To serve 8 to 10

6 tablespoons butter, softened, plus
  2 tablespoons butter, melted
2 cups finely chopped onions
1 teaspoon crumbled dried sage leaves
1 teaspoon salt
Freshly ground black pepper
4 pounds lean boneless pork, trimmed

of all fat and cut into ½-inch dice
4 medium-sized tart cooking apples
  (about 1½ pounds), peeled, cored
  and cut into ¼-inch slices
½ cup water
6 medium-sized boiling potatoes
  (about 2 pounds), peeled and cut
  into quarters
½ to ¾ cup milk

Preheat the oven to 325°. Using a pastry brush, coat the bottom and sides of a heavy 5- to 6-quart casserole with 2 tablespoons of the softened butter. In a small bowl, combine the chopped onions, sage, salt and a few grindings of pepper, and toss them about with a spoon until well mixed. Spread about one third of the diced pork in the casserole, strew with ½ cup of the onion mixture, top with half the apple slices, and sprinkle with another ½ cup of the onions. Repeat with layers of pork, onions and apples, and top with the remaining pork. Pour in the water, and bring to a boil on top of the stove. Cover the casserole tightly, and bake in the middle of the oven for 1½ hours, or until the pork is tender and shows no resistance when pierced with the tip of a small, sharp knife.

Meanwhile, drop the potatoes into enough lightly salted boiling water to cover them completely. Boil briskly, uncovered, until tender, then drain and return the potatoes to the pan. Shake over low heat until the potatoes are dry and mealy. Then mash them to a smooth purée with a fork, a potato ricer or an electric mixer. Beat in the remaining 4 tablespoons of softened butter and ½ cup of the milk, 2 tablespoons at a time. Use up to ¼ cup more milk if necessary to make a purée thick enough to hold its shape in a spoon. Beat in ½ teaspoon of salt and a few grindings of black pepper, taste for seasoning, and set aside.

When the pork is done, spread the mashed potatoes evenly over it with a spatula. Make an attractive pattern on the potatoes with the tines of a fork, and brush liberally with the melted butter. Bake in the upper third of the oven for about 10 minutes, or until the top of the pie has begun to brown. Slide under the broiler for a few seconds to give the potatoes a deeper color, and serve at once, directly from the casserole.

Steak-and-Kidney Pie

To serve 4 to 6

1½ pounds lean boneless sirloin or
    top round steak cut into 1-inch
    cubes
1 pound veal kidneys, peeled,
    trimmed of fat and cut into 1-
    inch cubes
2 teaspoons salt
1 teaspoon freshly ground black
    pepper
¼ cup flour
¼ cup rendered beef suet or lard,
    or substitute 3 tablespoons butter
    combined with 1 tablespoon

vegetable oil
1 cup thinly sliced fresh mushrooms
    (about ¼ pound)
½ cup coarsely chopped onions
1½ cups water
¼ cup pale dry sherry or dry red
    wine
1 tablespoon finely chopped parsley
¼ teaspoon thyme
¼ teaspoon Worcestershire sauce
Rough puff pastry *(page 75)*
1 egg yolk combined with 1
    tablespoon heavy cream

Preheat the oven to 425°. Pat the cubes of steak and kidney completely dry with paper towels, and sprinkle them with 1 teaspoon of the salt and ½ teaspoon of the pepper. In a bowl, combine the cubes with the flour, tossing them about with a spoon to coat them evenly.

In a heavy 10- to 12-inch skillet, heat the fat until it splutters. Brown a dozen or so of the cubes at a time over high heat, turning them frequently and regulating the heat so that the meat colors quickly and evenly without burning. Add more fat to the pan when necessary. With a slotted spoon, transfer the cubes to a heavy 2-quart casserole about 4 inches deep.

Add the mushrooms and chopped onions to the fat remaining in the skillet and cook over moderate heat, stirring constantly, for 2 or 3 minutes. With a slotted spoon, transfer the mushrooms and onions to the casserole. Pour the water into the skillet and bring it to a boil over high heat, meanwhile scraping in any brown particles clinging to the bottom and sides of the pan. Pour it over the meat in the casserole and add the sherry, parsley, thyme, Worcestershire sauce, and the remaining salt and pepper. Stir together gently.

On a lightly floured surface, roll the pastry out into a rough rectangle about ¼ inch thick, and cut 2 strips about 12 inches long and ½ inch wide from the ends. Lay the strips end to end around the rim of the casserole and press them firmly into place. Moisten them lightly with a pastry brush dipped in cold water. Then drape the remaining pastry over the rolling pin, lift it up, and carefully unroll it over the casserole. With a small knife or scissors, trim off the excess pastry, and secure the edges to the rim by crimping them tightly with your fingers or the tines of a fork. Reroll any scraps of pastry and cut them into simple flower and leaf shapes. Moisten their bottom sides with the egg-yolk-and-cream mixture and arrange them attractively on top of the pie.

Make 2 parallel cuts each about 1 inch long in the center of the pie and, with a pastry brush, paint the surface of the pie with the egg-yolk mixture.

Bake in the middle of the oven for 30 minutes, then reduce the heat to 350° and bake for another 30 minutes, or until the crust is golden brown. Serve at once, directly from the baking dish.

Chicken-and-Leek Pie

To serve 4 to 6

A 4- to 4½-pound roasting chicken or stewing fowl
1 large onion, peeled and quartered
1 small celery stalk including the leaves
A bouquet of 8 parsley sprigs and 1 small bay leaf, tied together
¼ teaspoon thyme
1 tablespoon salt
10 medium-sized leeks, including 1

inch of the green stems, split in half and cut crosswise into 1-inch pieces
¼ pound cooked smoked beef tongue, cut into ⅛-inch slices
1 tablespoon finely chopped parsley
Rough puff pastry *(page 75)*
1 egg yolk combined with 1 tablespoon heavy cream
¼ cup heavy cream

In a heavy 6- to 8-quart pot, combine the chicken or fowl, onion, celery stalk, bouquet of parsley and bay leaf, thyme and salt, and pour in enough cold water to cover the chicken by 1 inch. Bring to a boil over high heat, meanwhile skimming off all the foam and scum with a large spoon as they rise to the surface. Then reduce the heat to low and simmer partially covered until the bird is tender but not falling apart. (A roasting chicken should be done in about 1 hour; a stewing fowl may take as long as 2 hours or more, depending on its age and tenderness.)

Transfer the chicken to a plate and strain the stock through a fine sieve set over a bowl, pressing down hard on the vegetables and herbs with the back of a spoon before discarding them. Pour 2 cups of the stock into a heavy 2- to 3-quart saucepan and skim the surface of its fat. Add the leeks and bring to a boil over high heat. Then reduce the heat to low and simmer partially covered for 15 minutes, or until the leeks are tender.

With a small, sharp knife, remove the skin from the chicken and cut the meat away from the bones. Discard the skin and bones, cut the meat into 1-inch pieces, and arrange them evenly on the bottom of a 1½-quart casserole or baking dish at least 2 inches deep. Pour the leeks and their stock over the chicken and sprinkle lightly with salt. Arrange the slices of tongue side by side over the top, but leave a space about 1 inch square in the center. Sprinkle with the chopped parsley.

Preheat the oven to 400°. On a lightly floured surface roll out the puff past-

Continued on next page

ry into a rough rectangle about ¼ inch thick. Then cut 2 strips, each about 12 inches long and ½ inch wide, from the ends. Lay the strips end to end around the rim of the baking dish and press them firmly into place. Moisten them lightly with a pastry brush dipped in cold water.

Drape the remaining pastry over the rolling pin, lift it up, and unfold it over the baking dish. Trim off the excess with a small, sharp knife and, with the tines of a fork or your fingers, crimp the pastry to secure it to the rim of the dish.

Gather the scraps of pastry into a ball, reroll and cut them into simple leaf and flower shapes; moisten one side with the egg-yolk-and-cream mixture and arrange them decoratively on the pie. Then brush the entire pastry surface with the remaining egg-yolk-and-cream mixture and cut a 1-inch round hole in the center of the pie.

Bake the pie in the middle of the oven for 1 hour, or until the crust is golden brown. Just before serving, heat the ¼ cup of cream to lukewarm and pour it through the hole in the crust.

Game Pie

To serve 4 to 6

2 tablespoons butter, softened, plus 2 tablespoons butter	Freshly ground black pepper
	4 slices lean bacon
2 one-pound partridges, quartered, or substitute 2 one-pound grouse, pheasant, woodcock or other gamebirds	¼ pound mushrooms, coarsely chopped
	1 tablespoon coarsely chopped shallots, or substitute 1 tablespoon coarsely chopped scallions
2 tablespoons vegetable oil	
1¼ cups chicken stock, fresh or canned	1 tablespoon finely chopped parsley
	2 teaspoons grated lemon peel
¾ pound veal scallops, cut ¼ inch thick	½ recipe rough puff pastry *(page 75)*
Salt	1 egg lightly beaten with 1 tablespoon milk

Preheat the oven to 425°. Using a pastry brush, coat the bottom and sides of a 1½-quart casserole or baking dish at least 2 inches deep with the 2 tablespoons of softened butter and set aside.

Wash the partridges under cold running water and pat the pieces completely dry with paper towels. In a heavy 10- to 12-inch skillet, melt the remaining 2 tablespoons of butter in the 2 tablespoons of oil over moderately high heat. When the foam begins to subside, brown the partridges a few pieces at a time, starting them skin side down and turning them with tongs. As the pieces become a deep golden brown, remove them to a plate.

Pour the stock into the skillet and bring it to a boil over high heat, meanwhile scraping in any brown particles clinging to the bottom and sides of the pan. Boil briskly for a minute or so; set the skillet aside off the heat.

Line the bottom of the baking dish with the veal scallops, sprinkle them with salt and a few grindings of pepper, and lay the bacon slices side by side over the veal. Arrange the partridge pieces skin side up on top. Mix the mushrooms, shallots, parsley, lemon peel, 1/4 teaspoon of salt and a few grindings of pepper together in a bowl and spread the mixture evenly over the partridge. Pour in the stock that you had set aside.

On a lightly floured surface roll the pastry out into a rough rectangle no more than 1/8 inch thick. Then cut two strips, each about 12 inches long and 1/2 inch wide, from the ends. Lay the strips end to end around the rim of the baking dish and press them firmly into place. Moisten them lightly with a pastry brush dipped in cold water.

Drape the remaining pastry over the rolling pin, lift it up, and unfold it over the baking dish. Trim off the excess with a small, sharp knife and, with the tines of a fork or your fingers, crimp the pastry to secure it to the rim of the dish.

Gather the scraps of pastry into a ball, reroll and cut them into simple leaf and flower shapes; moisten one side with the egg-and-milk mixture and arrange them decoratively on the pie. Then brush the entire pastry surface with the remaining egg-and-milk mixture, and cut a 1-inch round hole in the center of the pie.

Bake the pie in the middle of the oven for 20 minutes, reduce the heat to 375° and bake for 40 minutes longer, or until the crust is golden brown. Serve at once directly from the baking dish.

Eel Pie

To serve 4 to 6

3 pounds eel, cleaned and cut
crosswise into 2-inch slices
1 small onion, peeled and cut into
quarters, plus ½ cup thinly sliced
onion
4 small bay leaves
4 parsley sprigs plus 1 tablespoon
finely chopped parsley
4 tablespoons butter

1 cup pale dry sherry
¼ teaspoon ground nutmeg
⅛ teaspoon cayenne pepper
½ teaspoon salt
3 tablespoons flour
4 tablespoons fresh lemon juice
3 hard-cooked eggs, quartered
Rough puff pastry *(page 75)*
1 egg yolk combined with 1
tablespoon heavy cream

In a heavy 3- to 4-quart saucepan combine the eel, quartered onion, bay leaves and parsley sprigs, and cover with water. Bring to a boil over high heat, reduce the heat to low, partially cover the pan, and simmer for 20 minutes, or until the eel is firm to the touch. Do not overcook. With a slotted spoon, transfer the eel to a plate and strain the stock through a fine sieve into a bowl. Discard the vegetables. When the eel is cool enough to handle, remove the skin and cut the flesh away from the bones. Spread the pieces side by side in a 6-by-6-by-2-inch casserole or baking dish and set aside.

Preheat the oven to 450°. In a heavy 8- to 10-inch skillet, melt 1 tablespoon of the butter over moderate heat. When the foam begins to subside, add the sliced onion and cook, stirring frequently, for 5 minutes, or until the slices are soft and transparent but not brown. Add the sherry, chopped parsley, nutmeg, cayenne pepper and salt, and set aside off the heat.

In another 8- to 10-inch skillet, melt the remaining 3 tablespoons of butter over moderate heat. When the foam begins to subside, stir in the flour and mix thoroughly. Pour in 2 cups of the reserved eel stock and, stirring constantly with a whisk, cook over high heat until the sauce thickens heavily and comes to a boil. Reduce the heat to low and simmer for about 3 minutes to remove any taste of raw flour. Then add the lemon juice and the reserved onion-sherry mixture. Taste for seasoning. Pour the sauce over the eel slices, arrange the quartered eggs on top, and let the sauce cool to room temperature.

On a lightly floured surface, roll the puff pastry into a rough square about ¼ inch thick. Drape the pastry over the rolling pin, lift it up and unfold it over the baking dish. Trim off the excess with a small, sharp knife and, with the tines of a fork or your fingers, crimp the pastry to secure it to the rim of the dish. Gather the scraps of pastry into a ball, reroll and cut them into simple leaf and flower shapes. Moisten their bottom sides lightly with the egg-yolk-and-cream mixture, and arrange them decoratively on the pie. Then brush the entire pastry surface with the remaining egg-yolk-and-cream mixture and cut 3 parallel 1-inch slits ½ inch apart in the top.

Bake the pie in the middle of the oven for 15 minutes, then reduce the heat to 325° and bake for 30 minutes longer, or until the top is golden brown. Serve at once.

Cornish Pasty
To make 16 six-inch pasties

1 tablespoon butter, softened

Preheat the oven to 400°. Using a pastry brush, coat a large baking sheet with the 1 tablespoon of softened butter. Set aside.

PASTRY
4 cups all-purpose flour
1/8 teaspoon salt

1½ cups lard (¾ pound), chilled
   and cut into ¼-inch bits
8 to 10 tablespoons ice water

In a large chilled bowl, combine the flour, salt and lard. Working quickly, rub the flour and fat together with your fingertips until they look like coarse meal. Pour in 8 tablespoons of ice water all at once, toss together, and gather the dough into a ball. If the dough crumbles, add up to 2 tablespoons of water, 1 teaspoonful at a time, until the particles adhere. Dust the pastry with a little flour and wrap it in wax paper. Refrigerate for at least 1 hour.

On a lightly floured surface, roll out the dough into a circle about ¼ inch thick. With a pastry wheel or sharp knife, cut the dough into 6-inch rounds using a small plate or pot lid as a guide. Gather the scraps together into a ball, roll it out again, and cut it into 6-inch rounds as before.

FILLING
1 cup coarsely chopped white or
   yellow turnips
2 cups finely diced lean boneless
   beef, preferably top round
1 cup coarsely chopped onions

2 cups finely diced potatoes
1½ teaspoons salt
1 teaspoon freshly ground black
   pepper
1 egg, lightly beaten

With a large spoon, toss the turnips, beef, onions, potatoes, salt and pepper together. Place about ¼ cup of the mixture in the center of each pastry round. Moisten the edges of the rounds with a pastry brush dipped in cold water, then fold the rounds in half to enclose the filling completely. Press the seams together firmly and crimp them with your fingers or the tines of a fork. Place the pasties on the baking sheet, and cut two slits about 1 inch long in the top of each. Brush lightly with the beaten egg and bake in the middle of the oven for 15 minutes. Reduce the heat to 350° and bake for 30 minutes, or until the pasties are golden brown. Serve hot or at room temperature.

Fish Pie

To serve 4 to 6

6 medium-sized baking potatoes (about 2 pounds), peeled and cut into quarters
7 tablespoons butter, softened, plus 2 tablespoons butter, cut into ¼-inch bits
1½ to 1¾ cups milk
1 teaspoon salt
Freshly ground black pepper
12 raw medium-sized shrimp
2 medium-sized onions, peeled and thinly sliced

3 tablespoons flour
¼ cup heavy cream
3 tablespoons finely chopped parsley
2 teaspoons anchovy paste
¼ teaspoon dried fennel seeds
Pinch of cayenne pepper
½ pound of fillets of any firm white fish such as sole, haddock or flounder, cut into 2-inch pieces
½ pound fresh or thoroughly defrosted frozen crab meat, or substitute one 7½-ounce can crab meat, thoroughly drained

Drop the potatoes into enough lightly salted boiling water to cover them completely. Boil briskly, uncovered, until tender. Drain and return the potatoes to the pan. Shake over low heat until they are dry and mealy. Then mash them to a smooth purée with a fork, a potato ricer or an electric mixer. Beat in 4 tablespoons of the butter and ½ cup of the milk, 2 tablespoons at a time. Use up to ¼ cup more milk if necessary to make a purée just thick enough to hold its shape in a spoon. Beat in the salt and a few grindings of black pepper, taste for seasoning, and set aside.

Shell the shrimp, and devein them by making a shallow incision down their backs with a small knife and lifting out their intestinal veins. Wash the shrimp under cold running water, and pat them dry with paper towels.

Preheat the oven to 400°. In a heavy 10- to 12-inch skillet, melt 3 tablespoons of the butter over moderate heat. When the foam has almost subsided, add the onions and cook, stirring frequently, for 5 minutes, or until they are soft and transparent but not brown. Thoroughly mix in the flour, pour in the remaining 1 cup of milk and the cream, and bring to a boil over high heat, stirring constantly with a whisk until the sauce is smooth and thick. Add the parsley, anchovy paste, fennel seeds and cayenne pepper, and stir until the anchovy paste dissolves. Then add the shrimp, fish and crab meat, and simmer slowly for about 5 minutes. Taste for seasoning, and pour the entire contents of the skillet into a 4- to 5-quart baking dish.

Spread the mashed potatoes evenly over the fish and smooth the top with a spatula. Make an attractive pattern on the potatoes with the tines of a fork, and dot with the remaining 2 tablespoons of butter cut into bits. Bake in the middle of the oven for about 20 minutes, or until the top of the pie is a light golden brown. Slide under the broiler for a few seconds to give the crust a deeper color, and serve at once directly from the baking dish.

Sweet Puddings and Pies

Rough Puff Pastry

2 cups sifted all-purpose flour
¼ teaspoon salt
¼ pound (1 stick) unsalted butter, thoroughly chilled and cut into

¼-inch bits
¼ cup lard, thoroughly chilled and cut into ¼-inch bits
4 to 6 tablespoons ice water

Sift the flour and salt together into a large chilled mixing bowl. Drop in the butter and lard and, working quickly, use your fingertips to rub the flour and fat together until the mixture looks like flakes of coarse meal. Pour 4 tablespoons of ice water over the mixture all at once, and gather the dough into a ball.

If the dough crumbles, add up to 2 tablespoons more ice water, 1 teaspoon at a time, until the particles adhere. Dust lightly with flour, wrap the dough in wax paper and chill for 30 minutes.

Place the pastry on a lightly floured board or table, and press it into a rectangular shape about 1 inch thick. Dust a little flour over and under it, and roll it out into a strip about 21 inches long and 6 inches wide. Fold the strip into thirds to form a 3-layered rectangular packet, reducing its dimensions to about 7 by 6 inches.

Turn the pastry around so that an open end faces you and roll it out once more to a 21-by-6-inch strip. Fold it into thirds as before and roll it out again to a similar strip. Repeat this entire process twice more, ending with the pastry folded into a packet.

Wrap the pastry tightly in wax paper, foil or a plastic bag, and refrigerate it for at least 1 hour. The pastry may be kept in the refrigerator for 3 or 4 days before it is used.

Short-Crust Pastry

6 tablespoons unsalted butter, chilled and cut into ¼-inch bits
2 tablespoons lard, chilled and cut into ¼-inch bits

1½ cups all-purpose flour
¼ teaspoon salt
1 tablespoon sugar
3 to 4 tablespoons ice water

In a large, chilled bowl, combine the butter, lard, flour, salt and sugar. With your fingertips rub the flour and fat together until they look like coarse meal. Do not let the mixture become oily. Pour 3 tablespoons of ice water over the mixture all at once, toss together lightly, and gather the dough into a ball. If the dough crumbles, add up to 1 tablespoon more ice water by drops until the particles adhere. Dust the pastry with a little flour and wrap it in wax paper. Refrigerate for at least 1 hour before using.

NOTE: If you are not making a sweet pastry, substitute ½ teaspoon salt for the ¼ teaspoon salt and the 1 tablespoon sugar in the recipe above.

Apple Dumplings
To make 6 dumplings

4 tablespoons butter, softened
5 tablespoons dark-brown sugar
3 tablespoons fresh lemon juice
2 teaspoons finely grated lemon peel
3 tablespoons dried currants
¼ teaspoon ground cinnamon

A double recipe of short-crust pastry (above)
6 large, firm tart cooking apples
Water
6 teaspoons sugar
Custard sauce (page 96) or whipped cream

Preheat the oven to 375°. Using a pastry brush, coat a large baking sheet with 1 tablespoon of the softened butter. In a mixing bowl, cream the remaining 3 tablespoons of butter and the brown sugar together by beating and mashing them against the sides of the bowl with a large spoon until they are light and fluffy. Beat in the lemon juice, lemon peel, currants and cinnamon. Set aside.

On a lightly floured surface, roll out half the pastry into a circle about ¼ inch thick. With a pastry wheel or sharp knife, cut the dough into 8-inch rounds using a small plate or pot lid as a guide. Roll the remaining half of the pastry into a circle and cut into 8-inch rounds as before.

Peel and core each apple, and pack each cavity tightly with about 2 tablespoons of the currant mixture. Place the apple in the center of a pastry round and bring the pastry up around it, twisting the edges tightly together at the top.

Arrange the dumplings, seam side up, on the baking sheet, and bake in the middle of the oven for 20 minutes. With a pastry brush, moisten the tops of the dumplings with water, and sprinkle each one with 1 teaspoon of the sugar. Return to the oven and bake for 5 to 10 minutes, or until the sugar is glazed and the pastry is golden brown. Serve at once, accompanied by custard sauce or whipped cream.

Mince Pies

To make eight 2½-inch pies

| | Short-crust pastry *(opposite)* |
| 8 teaspoons butter, softened | 1½ cups mincemeat *(page 7)* |

Preheat the oven to 375°. With a pastry brush, coat the bottom and sides of eight 2½-inch tart tins with the softened butter, allowing 1 teaspoon of butter for each tin. (These mince pies are most successful baked in specialized tart tins, available in well-stocked housewares stores; check the size by measuring the diameter of the bottom, not the top.)

On a lightly floured surface, roll out the pastry into a circle about ⅛ inch thick. With a cookie cutter or the rim of a glass, cut sixteen 3½-inch rounds of pastry. Gently press 8 of the rounds, 1 at a time, into the tart tins. Then spoon about 3 tablespoons of mincemeat into each pastry shell. With a pastry brush dipped in cold water, lightly moisten the outside edges of the pastry shells and carefully fit the remaining 8 rounds over them. Crimp the edges of the pastry together with your fingers or press them with the tines of a fork. Trim the excess pastry from around the rims with a sharp knife, and cut two ½-inch long parallel slits about ¼ inch apart in the top of each of the pies.

Arrange the pies on a large baking sheet, and bake them in the middle of the oven for 10 minutes. Reduce the heat to 350° and bake for 20 minutes longer, or until the crust is golden brown. Run the blade of a knife around the inside edges of the pies to loosen them slightly, and set them aside to cool in the pans. Then turn out the pies with a narrow spatula and serve.

NOTE: Mince pies are traditional Christmas fare, often served with whipped cream, Cumberland rum butter or brandy butter *(both in Recipe Index)*.

Blackberry-and-Apple Pie
To serve 6 to 8

3 medium-sized tart cooking apples (about 1 pound), peeled, cored and cut into ¼-inch-thick slices	3 pints ripe blackberries (about 2¼ pounds), washed and thoroughly drained
½ cup plus 3 tablespoons sugar	Short-crust pastry *(page 76)*
2 tablespoons butter, melted	1 tablespoon superfine sugar

Preheat the oven to 425°. In a heavy 8- to 10-inch skillet, combine the apples, 3 tablespoons of the sugar and the butter, and cook uncovered over moderate heat, stirring frequently, for 5 minutes, or until the apples are tender but not falling apart. Remove the pan from the heat and let the apples cool to room temperature.

Pack the blackberries snugly into the bottom of a round, deep pie dish about 7½ inches in diameter and 2½ inches deep, preferably a dish with a ½-inch-wide rim. Sprinkle the berries with ¼ cup of the sugar, adding up to ¼ cup of additional sugar to taste, and spread the cooled apple slices evenly over the top.

On a lightly floured surface, roll the pastry into a rough circle at least 10 inches in diameter and ⅛ inch thick. From the edge cut two strips about 12 inches long and ½ inch wide. Moisten the edge of the pie dish with a pastry brush or your finger dipped in cold water and lay the strips of pastry around it, overlapping the ends to secure them and pressing the strips firmly against the edge of the dish. Moisten the tops of the strips, then drape the remaining pastry over the rolling pin and unroll it over the dish. Press it gently in place. With scissors or a knife, trim the pastry to within ½ inch of the dish and fold the border into a roll around the rim. Press the tines of a fork all around the edges of the pastry to secure it to the dish. With a small, sharp knife, cut three 1-inch-long parallel slits about ½ inch apart in the center of the pie. Brush the top lightly with cold water and sprinkle it evenly with 1 tablespoon of superfine sugar. Bake in the middle of the oven for 25 minutes, or until the crust is golden brown. Serve the pie at once, directly from its baking dish, or let it cool to room temperature before serving. Blackberry-and-apple pie is traditionally accompanied by custard sauce *(Recipe Index)* or heavy cream.

NOTE: Like all English fruit pies, blackberry-and-apple has no pastry bottom and is very moist; it is eaten with a dessert spoon rather than a fork.

Custard Tart

To serve 6 to 8

1 tablespoon butter, softened
Short-crust pastry *(page 76)*
1½ cups milk

1 cup heavy cream
¼ cup sugar
4 eggs
1 teaspoon vanilla extract

Using a pastry brush, coat the bottom and sides of a 9-inch false-bottomed *quiche* or cake pan no more than 1¼ inches deep with the tablespoon of softened butter. Preheat the oven to 400°.

On a lightly floured board, pat the pastry dough into a rough circle about 1 inch thick, then roll it out into a circle about ⅛ inch thick and about 12 inches in diameter. Drape the pastry over the rolling pin; lift it up and unroll it slackly over the pan. Gently press the pastry into the sides of the pan, being careful not to stretch it. Roll the pin over the rim of the pan, pressing down hard to trim off the excess.

Spread a large sheet of buttered aluminum foil across the pan and press it gently into the pan to support the sides of the pastry shell. Bake in the middle of the oven for 10 minutes, then carefully lift out the foil. Return to the oven for 2 or 3 minutes. With the tip of a small, sharp knife, pierce any air bubbles in the pastry and bake for about 5 minutes longer, or until the shell is a delicate light brown. Remove from the oven and set the pan on a large jar or coffee can. Slip down the outside rim and slide the shell onto a rack to cool. Then place the shell on a baking sheet.

Reduce the oven heat to 375°. In a 1- to 1½-quart saucepan, heat the milk, cream and sugar, stirring until the sugar dissolves. When bubbles begin to form around the edge of the pan, remove from the heat. In a large bowl, beat the eggs with a whisk or a rotary or electric beater until they are well combined. Beating slowly, pour in the hot milk-and-cream mixture in a thin stream. Beat in the vanilla. Ladle the mixture into the pastry shell.

Bake the tart in the middle of the oven for 10 minutes. Then reduce the heat to 300° and bake for 20 to 30 minutes longer, or until a knife inserted in the center of the custard comes out clean. With a large spatula slide the tart onto a serving plate, and serve hot or at room temperature.

Treacle Tart

To make one 9-inch tart

6 tablespoons chilled butter, cut in ¼-inch bits, plus 1 tablespoon butter, softened
2 tablespoons chilled lard, cut in ¼-inch bits
1½ cups flour
1 teaspoon sugar
3 to 4 tablespoons ice water
1½ cups imported English golden syrup or 1½ cups light corn syrup

combined with 1 teaspoon molasses
1½ cups fresh soft crumbs, made from homemade-type white bread, pulverized in a blender or shredded with a fork
1 tablespoon fresh lemon juice
½ teaspoon ground ginger
1 egg, lightly beaten
Custard sauce *(page 96)*

In a large, chilled mixing bowl, combine the 6 tablespoons of chilled butter, lard, flour and sugar. With your fingertips rub the flour and fat together until they look like flakes of coarse, dry meal. Pour in 3 tablespoons of ice water all at once, toss together lightly and gather the dough into a ball. If the dough crumbles, add up to 1 tablespoon more ice water, a drop or two at a time, until the particles adhere. Dust the pastry with a little flour, wrap it in wax paper, and refrigerate for at least 1 hour.

Use a pastry brush to coat the bottom and sides of a 9-inch pie plate with 1 tablespoon of softened butter. Preheat the oven to 350°.

On a lightly floured surface, pat the dough into a rough circle about 1 inch thick, then roll it out into a circle about ⅛ inch thick and about 12 inches in diameter. Drape the pastry over the rolling pin, lift it up, and unroll it slackly over the pie plate. Gently press the pastry into the plate, but be careful not to stretch it. Roll the pin over the rim, pressing down hard to trim off the excess.

In a large bowl, combine the syrup, bread crumbs, lemon juice, ginger and egg. Stir until the ingredients are well combined, then pour the mixture into the pastry shell, smoothing it out with a spatula. The shell should be about two thirds full. Bake in the middle of the oven for 20 minutes, or until the filling is firm to the touch and the crust golden brown.

Cut the tart into wedges and serve at once directly from the pie plate, accompanied by the custard sauce served in a bowl.

Queen of Puddings
BAKED PUDDING WITH MERINGUE TOPPING

To serve 6 to 8

3 tablespoons butter, softened
1 lemon
2 cups milk
½ cup sugar
1 cup fresh soft crumbs, made from homemade-type white bread, trimmed of crusts and pulverized in a blender or shredded with a fork
3 egg yolks
3 egg whites
¼ cup raspberry jam
4 candied cherries, cut into halves

Preheat the oven to 350°. Using a pastry brush, evenly coat the bottom and sides of an 8-inch round pie plate about 1½ inches deep with 1 tablespoon of the softened butter. Set aside.

With a small, sharp knife or a vegetable peeler with a rotating blade, carefully remove the skin of the lemon without including any of the bitter white pith beneath it. Combine the lemon peel and milk in a heavy 1- to 1½-quart saucepan, and simmer over low heat for 4 or 5 minutes. Then remove and discard the peel. Add the remaining 2 tablespoons of butter and ¼ cup of the sugar to the milk, increase the heat to moderate, and cook, stirring constantly, until the sugar and butter dissolve. Remove the pan from the heat, stir in the bread crumbs and let the mixture cool to room temperature. Then beat in the egg yolks, one at a time, and pour the mixture into the pie plate. Smooth the top with a rubber spatula.

Bake the pudding in the middle of the oven for 20 minutes, or until it is firm throughout. Meanwhile, with a whisk or a rotary or electric beater, beat the egg whites until they foam. Then add the remaining ¼ cup of sugar and beat until the egg whites form stiff peaks on the beater when it is lifted out of the bowl.

Remove the pudding from the oven and let it cool for 4 or 5 minutes. Melt the jam over low heat, and pour it evenly over the top of the pudding. Spread the egg whites over the jam and arrange the cherry halves decoratively on top. Return the pudding to the oven and bake for 10 to 12 minutes, or until the top is a light golden brown.

Plum Pudding
To make 4 puddings

1½ cups dried currants
2 cups seedless raisins
2 cups white raisins
¾ cup finely chopped candied mixed fruit peel
¾ cup finely chopped candied cherries
1 cup blanched slivered almonds
1 medium-sized tart cooking apple, peeled, quartered, cored and coarsely chopped
1 small carrot, scraped and coarsely chopped
2 tablespoons finely grated orange peel

2 teaspoons finely grated lemon peel
½ pound finely chopped beef suet
2 cups all-purpose flour
4 cups fresh soft crumbs, made from homemade-type white bread, pulverized in a blender or shredded with a fork
1 cup dark-brown sugar
1 teaspoon ground allspice
1 teaspoon salt
6 eggs
1 cup brandy
⅓ cup fresh orange juice
¼ cup fresh lemon juice
½ cup brandy, for flaming (optional)

In a large, deep bowl, combine the currants, seedless raisins, white raisins, candied fruit peel, cherries, almonds, apple, carrot, orange and lemon peel, and beef suet, tossing them about with a spoon or your hands until well mixed. Stir in the flour, bread crumbs, brown sugar, allspice and salt.

In a separate bowl, beat the eggs until frothy. Stir in the 1 cup of brandy, the orange and lemon juice, and pour this mixture over the fruit mixture. Knead vigorously with both hands, then beat with a wooden spoon until all the ingredients are blended. Drape a dampened kitchen towel over the bowl and refrigerate for at least 12 hours.

Spoon the mixture into four 1-quart English pudding basins or plain molds, filling them to within 2 inches of their tops. Cover each mold with a strip of buttered foil, turning the edges down and pressing the foil tightly around the sides to secure it. Drape a dampened kitchen towel over each mold and tie it in place around the sides with a long piece of kitchen cord. Bring two opposite corners of the towel up to the top and knot them in the center of the mold; then bring up the remaining two corners and knot them similarly.

Place the molds in a large pot and pour in enough boiling water to come about three fourths of the way up their sides. Bring the water to a boil over high heat, cover the pot tightly, reduce the heat to its lowest point and steam the puddings for 8 hours. As the water in the steamer boils away, replenish it with additional boiling water.

When the puddings are done, remove them from the water and let them cool to room temperature. Then remove the towels and foil and re-cover the molds tightly with fresh foil. Refrigerate the puddings for at least 3 weeks before serving. Plum puddings may be kept up to a year in the refrigerator or other cool place; traditionally, they were often made a year in advance.

To serve, place the mold in a pot and pour in enough boiling water to come about three fourths of the way up the sides of the mold. Bring to a boil over high heat, cover the pot, reduce the heat to low and steam for 2 hours. Run a knife around the inside edges of the mold and place an inverted serving plate over it. Grasping the mold and plate firmly together, turn them over. The pudding should slide out easily.

Christmas pudding is traditionally accompanied by Cumberland rum butter or brandy butter *(Recipe Index)*. Small paper-wrapped coins (such as sixpences and threepenny bits) are sometimes pressed into the pudding as good-luck pieces just before it is served.

If you would like to set the pudding aflame before you serve it, warm the ½ cup of brandy in a small saucepan over low heat, ignite it with a match and pour it flaming over the pudding.

Bread-and-Butter Pudding

To serve 6 to 8

	⅛ teaspoon ground cinnamon
8 tablespoons butter, softened	5 eggs
12 thin slices homemade-type white	3 cups milk
bread	1 cup heavy cream
½ cup dried currants	¼ cup sugar
½ cup white raisins	A pinch of nutmeg

With a pastry brush, coat the bottom and sides of a 7-by-10-by-2½-inch baking dish with 2 tablespoons of the butter.

Trim and discard the crusts from the bread, and butter it liberally on both sides. Place 4 slices of the bread side by side on the bottom of the dish, and trim them to fit snugly. Toss the currants, raisins and cinnamon together in a small bowl, and strew half of the mixture over the bread. Add a second layer of bread, strew the remainder of the fruit over it, and top with a final layer of bread.

With a whisk or a rotary or electric beater, beat the eggs to a froth in a large mixing bowl. Beat in the milk, cream, sugar and nutmeg, and then pour the mixture evenly over the bread. Let the pudding rest at room temperature for at least 30 minutes, or until the bread has absorbed almost all of the liquid.

Preheat the oven to 350°. Cover the pudding with a lightly buttered sheet of foil and bake in the middle of the oven for 30 minutes. Then remove the foil and bake for 30 minutes longer, or until the top is crisp and golden brown. Serve hot, directly from the baking dish.

Cabinet Pudding

RICH CUSTARD-AND-SPONGECAKE DESSERT

To serve 6 to 8

	wide and 3 inches long
2 tablespoons butter, softened	¼ cup Madeira
¼ cup candied cherries	3 eggs
¼ cup candied angelica, cut into 1-	3 tablespoons sugar
inch strips	1 cup milk
⅓ cup seedless raisins	½ cup heavy cream
18 ladyfingers, each about 1 inch	¼ cup flour

Using a pastry brush, coat the bottom and sides of a 1½-quart English pudding basin or charlotte mold with 1 tablespoon of the softened butter. Refrigerate for 10 minutes. Slice a cherry in half, place it cut side up in the center of the mold, and arrange 8 strips of the angelica in a spokelike pattern around it. Decorate the sides of the basin with 6 to 8 rows of raisins, arranging them so that the rows reach about 4 inches up the sides of the mold. (The chilled butter should hold the raisins in place; if it doesn't, chill the mold a few minutes longer.)

Now, line the mold with ladyfingers in the following fashion: Split 9 ladyfingers in half, and place 3 or 4 of the halves, cut side up, on the bottom of the mold. Sprinkle with 2 tablespoons of the Madeira. Stand 14 or 15 ladyfinger halves, cut side in, around the inside of the mold, overlapping them slightly to line the sides completely.

Cut the remaining angelica and cherries into ¼-inch dice and combine them with the remaining raisins in a small bowl. Stir in 1 tablespoon of Madeira and set aside.

For the custard, beat the eggs and sugar together with a whisk, rotary or electric beater, for about 3 or 4 minutes, or until the mixture is thick. Gradually beat in the milk and the cream.

Assemble the pudding in the following fashion: Sprinkle the bottom layer of ladyfingers with a tablespoon of the diced fruits and pour over it ½ cup of the custard mixture. Break 4 ladyfingers into coarse pieces 1 inch square; spread half of them on the custard, sprinkle with a tablespoon of Madeira, and arrange about ⅓ of the diced fruit on top. Add another cup of the custard, cover with the rest of the ladyfinger pieces and spread them with the remaining diced fruit. Pour in the remaining custard and place the remaining ladyfingers, halved, on top. Sprinkle with the rest of the Madeira.

Cut out a circle of wax paper 2 inches larger in diameter than that of the mold and, with a pastry brush, coat it with the remaining tablespoon of soft butter. Place the wax paper, buttered side down, over the mold, and turn down the edges to hold it securely in place. Moisten a kitchen towel with cold water, wring it dry, and sprinkle it evenly with the flour. Shake the towel to remove the excess, and drape it, floured side down, over the top of the mold. Bring the ends of the towel down around the sides of the mold, and tie the towel in place about 1½ to 2 inches down the side with a long length of kitchen cord. Bring up two diagonally opposite corners of the towel and tie them together on top of the pudding. Then bring the remaining corners together and tie them similarly.

Place the pudding in a large, heavy pot or saucepan, and pour in enough boiling water to come three fourths of the way up the side of the mold. Bring to a boil over high heat, cover the pot tightly, reduce the heat to its lowest point, and steam for 1¼ hours. Do not let the water come to a boil again; if necessary place an asbestos mat under the pot. Replenish the water in the steamer with more boiling water as it boils away.

To serve, remove the towel and paper. Wipe the outside of the mold dry and let the pudding rest for 2 or 3 minutes. Then place an inverted plate over the top, grasp the edges of the mold and plate together firmly, and turn them over quickly. The pudding should slide out easily. If any raisins or bits of fruit cling to the mold, return them to their original position on the pudding. Serve the pudding warm.

Fresh Fruit Fool
PURÉED FRUIT DESSERT

To serve 6 to 8

	1½ pounds)
1 quart fresh ripe gooseberries,	1 cup sugar
raspberries or blackberries (about	3 cups heavy cream

Pick over the berries carefully, removing any stems and discarding berries that are badly bruised or show signs of mold. Place the fruit in a heavy 3- to 4-quart saucepan and cook over low heat for 30 minutes, stirring and mashing the fruit against the bottom and sides of the pan to extract its juices. Stir in the sugar and simmer until dissolved. Taste and add more sugar if desired. Then purée the fruit, a cup or so at a time, in a blender, or force it through a fine sieve or food mill set over a bowl. Cover and refrigerate.

Just before serving, beat the cream with a whisk or a rotary or electric beater until it forms stiff peaks on the beater when it is lifted from the bowl. With a rubber spatula gently fold the puréed fruit into the cream but do not overmix; the intermingled streaks of purée and cream should create a marbled effect. Serve at once in parfait glasses or individual dessert bowls.

Crowdie Cream
OATMEAL AND RUM DESSERT

To serve 4

⅓ cup regular oatmeal	3 tablespoons confectioners' sugar
1 cup heavy cream	2 tablespoons dark rum

Preheat the oven to 400°. Spread the oatmeal evenly over the bottom of a 9- or 10-inch layer-cake pan, and toast in the middle of the oven, shaking the pan occasionally, for about 15 minutes, or until the flakes are a rich golden brown. Watch carefully for any sign of burning and regulate the heat accordingly. Set aside to cool.

In a large chilled bowl, whip the cream with a whisk or a rotary or electric beater until it begins to thicken. Add the confectioners' sugar and beat until the cream is firm enough to form unwavering peaks on the beater when it is lifted out of the bowl. Lightly stir in the rum, a tablespoon or so at a time. Then, with a rubber spatula, gently but thoroughly fold in the toasted oatmeal, using an over-under cutting motion rather than a stirring motion. Pile the cream into chilled individual serving bowls or into parfait glasses and serve it at once.

NOTE: In Scotland, crowdie cream was traditionally served as a dessert on Shrove Tuesday. A ring was sometimes hidden in the cream as a charm predicting marriage for the finder.

Burnt Cream
CARAMEL CREAM DESSERT

To serve 6 to 8

6 egg yolks	3 cups heavy cream
6 tablespoons sugar	1 tablespoon vanilla extract

Preheat the oven to 350°. With a whisk or a rotary or electric beater, beat the egg yolks and 2 tablespoons of the sugar together in a mixing bowl for 3 or 4 minutes, or until the yolks are thick and pale yellow.

Heat the cream in a heavy 1½- to 2-quart saucepan until small bubbles begin to form around the edges of the pan. Then, beating constantly, pour the cream in a slow stream into the beaten egg yolks. Add the vanilla extract and strain the mixture through a fine sieve into a 1-quart soufflé dish or other baking dish 6 to 7 inches in diameter and at least 2 inches deep.

Place the dish in a large shallow pan on the middle shelf of the oven and pour enough boiling water into the pan to come halfway up the sides of the dish. Bake for about 45 minutes, or until a knife inserted in the center comes out clean. Remove the dish from the water and cool to room temperature. Refrigerate for at least 4 hours, or until the cream is thoroughly chilled.

About 2 hours before serving, preheat the broiler to its highest point. Sprinkle the top of the cream with the remaining 4 tablespoons of sugar, coating the surface as evenly as possible. Slide the dish under the broiler about 3 inches from the heat, and cook for 4 or 5 minutes, or until the sugar forms a crust over the cream. Watch carefully for any signs of burning and regulate the heat accordingly. Cool the cream to room temperature, then refrigerate it again until ready to serve.

Trifle
CAKE, FRUIT AND CUSTARD DESSERT WITH WHIPPED CREAM

To serve 6 to 8

A piece of homemade poundcake about 5 inches long, 4 inches wide and 3 inches high, or substitute a 12-ounce packaged poundcake
4 tablespoons raspberry jam
1 cup blanched almonds, separated into halves

1 cup medium-dry sherry
¼ cup brandy
2 cups heavy cream
2 tablespoons superfine sugar
A double recipe of custard sauce (page 96), chilled slightly
2 cups fresh raspberries, or 2 ten-ounce packages frozen raspberries, defrosted and thoroughly drained

Cut the poundcake into 1-inch-thick slices and spread them with the raspberry jam. Place 2 or 3 of the cake slices, jam side up, in the bottom of a glass serving bowl 8 or 9 inches across and 3 inches deep. Cut the remaining slices of cake into 1-inch cubes, scatter them over the slices, and sprinkle ½ cup of the almonds on top. Then pour in the sherry and brandy and let the mixture steep at room temperature for at least 30 minutes.

In a large chilled bowl, whip the cream with a whisk or a rotary or electric beater until it thickens slightly. Add the sugar and continue to beat until the cream is stiff enough to form unwavering peaks on the beater when it is lifted out of the bowl.

To assemble the trifle, set 10 of the best berries aside and scatter the rest over the cake. With a spatula spread the custard across the top. Then gently smooth half of the whipped cream over the surface of the custard. Using a pastry bag fitted with a large rose tip, pipe the remaining whipped cream decoratively around the edge. Garnish the cream with the 10 reserved berries and the remaining ½ cup of almonds.

The trifle will be at its best served at once, but it may be refrigerated for an hour or two.

Syllabub

WHIPPED-CREAM-AND-WINE DESSERT

To serve 8

	preferably superfine
16 macaroons	1 teaspoon finely grated lemon peel
⅓ cup Madeira	A pinch of ground cinnamon
¼ cup fresh lemon juice	½ teaspoon almond extract
6 tablespoons sugar,	2 cups heavy cream

Crumble two macaroons into each of eight 1-cup parfait or sherbet glasses. Set aside.

In a large chilled bowl, combine the Madeira, lemon juice, sugar, lemon peel, cinnamon and almond extract, and stir until the sugar dissolves. Pour in the cream and beat with a whisk or a rotary or electric beater until it forms stiff peaks on the beater when it is lifted from the bowl. Pile the cream on top of the macaroons and chill for at least 30 minutes before serving.

Jam Sponge

STEAMED JAM PUDDING

To serve 4 to 6

1 tablespoon plus 4 tablespoons butter, softened	½ cup milk
¼ cup sugar	½ teaspoon double-acting baking powder
2 tablespoons plus 1¼ cups flour	A pinch of salt
2 eggs	½ cup raspberry jam

Using a pastry brush, coat the bottom and sides of a 6-cup English pudding basin or plain mold with 1 tablespoon of the softened butter. Set aside.

In a large mixing bowl, cream the remaining butter, sugar and 2 table-spoons of the flour together by mashing and beating them against the sides of the bowl with a spoon until they are light and fluffy. Beat in the eggs, one at a time, and then add the milk. Combine the remaining 1¼ cups of flour with the baking powder and salt and sift it gradually into the batter, beating constantly.

Spread the raspberry jam on the bottom of the mold and pour in the batter. Cover with a lid or with a circle of lightly buttered paper. Tie a damp, floured towel around the mold, following the procedure described in the recipe for steak-and-kidney pudding *(page 66)*.

Place the mold in a large pot or saucepan and pour in enough boiling water to come about three fourths of the way up the sides of the mold.

Bring the water to a boil over high heat, cover the pot tightly, then reduce the heat to its lowest point, and steam the pudding for 1½ hours. Do not let the water come to a boil again; if necessary place an asbestos mat under the pot. Replenish the water in the steamer with additional boiling water as it cooks away.

To unmold and serve the pudding, remove the lid or paper cover and the towel, and wipe the outside of the mold dry. Run a knife around the inside edges of the mold and place an inverted serving plate over it. Grasping the mold and plate firmly together, turn them over. The pudding should slide out easily. Serve it at once, accompanied, if you like, with hot custard sauce *(page 96)*.

Marmalade Pudding
To serve 6 to 8

5 tablespoons butter, softened
1 cup all-purpose flour
1½ teaspoons baking powder
½ teaspoon ground cinnamon
¼ teaspoon salt
⅔ cup sugar

2 eggs, lightly beaten
¼ cup milk combined with ¼ cup water
1 teaspoon finely grated orange peel
1 teaspoon vanilla extract
1 cup orange marmalade, preferably imported Seville orange marmalade

Preheat the oven to 350°. Using a pastry brush, coat the bottom and sides of a 9-by-5-by-3-inch loaf pan with 1 tablespoon of the softened butter. Sift the flour, baking powder, cinnamon and salt into a small bowl, and set aside.

In a large mixing bowl, cream the remaining 4 tablespoons of butter and the sugar together, beating and mashing them against the sides of the bowl with a spoon until they are light and fluffy. Beat in the eggs. Then beat in the sifted flour mixture, ¼ cup at a time, moistening the mixture after each addition with a little of the combined milk and water. Continue beating until all the ingredients are combined and the batter is smooth. Then beat in the orange peel and vanilla.

Stirring constantly, melt the marmalade over low heat in a small pan; then pour it into the loaf pan. Pour in the batter, and bake in the middle of the oven for 40 to 50 minutes, or until a cake tester inserted in the center of the pudding comes out clean.

Cool the pudding in the pan for about 10 minutes. Then run a long, sharp knife around the inside edges of the pan. Place an inverted serving plate over the pan and, grasping the pan and plate firmly together, quickly turn them over. The pudding should slide out easily. Serve warm, accompanied, if you like, with hot custard sauce *(page 96)*.

Summer Pudding
FRUIT-FILLED BREAD PUDDING

To serve 6 to 8

2 quarts (about 3 pounds) fresh
  ripe raspberries, blackberries,
  blueberries or red currants

1¼ cups superfine sugar
10 to 12 slices homemade-type white
  bread
1 cup heavy cream

Pick over the fruit carefully, removing any stems or caps and discarding any berries that are badly bruised or show signs of mold. Wash in a colander under cold running water, then shake the berries dry and spread them out on paper towels to drain. Place the berries in a large mixing bowl, sprinkle with the 1¼ cups of sugar, and toss them about gently with a large spoon until the sugar dissolves completely. Taste, and add more sugar if necessary. Cover tightly and set the berries aside.

With a small, sharp knife, cut 1 slice of bread into a circle or octagon so that it will exactly fit the bottom of a 2-quart English pudding basin, a 2-quart deep bowl, or a charlotte mold, and set it in place. Trim 6 or 7 slices of the bread into truncated wedge shapes 3½ to 4 inches wide across the top and about 3 inches wide across the bottom. Stand the wedges of bread, narrow end down, around the inner surface of the mold, overlapping them by about ¼ inch. Ladle the fruit mixture into the mold, and cover the top completely with the remaining bread. Cover the top of the mold with a flat plate, and on it set a 3- to 4-pound kitchen weight, or a heavy pan or casserole. Refrigerate the pudding for at least 12 hours, until the bread is completely saturated with the fruit syrup.

To remove the pudding from the mold, place a chilled serving plate upside down over it and, grasping the plate and mold firmly together, quickly invert them. The pudding should slide out easily. In a large chilled bowl, beat the cream with a whisk or a rotary or electric beater until it holds its shape softly. Serve the whipped cream separately with the pudding.

NOTE: If the berries are not fully ripened and soft, combine the fruit and sugar in a heavy 3- to 4-quart saucepan, and cook over low heat for about 5 minutes, shaking the pan frequently.

Speech House Pudding
To serve 4 to 6

2 tablespoons plus ¼ pound butter,
   softened
¼ cup sugar
4 egg yolks
1 cup all-purpose flour

¾ cup raspberry jam
4 egg whites
1 teaspoon baking soda dissolved
   in 2 tablespoons milk
Custard sauce *(page 96)*

With a pastry brush, coat the bottom and sides of a 1-quart English pudding basin or a 1-quart plain mold with 1 tablespoon of the softened butter. Set aside.

In a large bowl, cream ¼ pound of the softened butter and the sugar together by beating and mashing them against the sides of the bowl until they are light and fluffy. Beat in the egg yolks, one at a time. Then add the flour, ½ cup at a time, beating well after each addition. Beat in ¼ cup of the raspberry jam.

With a whisk, or a rotary or electric beater, beat the egg whites until they form unwavering peaks on the beater when it is lifted out of the bowl. Quickly stir the soda-and-milk mixture into the batter, then gently but thoroughly fold in the egg whites using an over-under cutting motion rather than a stirring motion. Spoon the mixture into the pudding basin or mold, and cover tightly with a lid or a lightly buttered sheet of foil.

Place the mold on a rack in a large, deep pot, and add enough boiling water to come halfway up the sides of the mold. Again bring the water to a boil over high heat, cover the pot tightly, and reduce the heat to low. Simmer for 2 hours, replenishing the water in the pot with more boiling water as necessary.

Remove the pudding from the water and let it rest for a minute or so. Then remove the lid or foil, and place an inverted plate over the basin or mold. Grasping plate and mold firmly together, quickly turn them over. The pudding should slide out easily. Over high heat, melt the remaining ½ cup of raspberry jam in a small saucepan and pour it over the pudding. Serve at once, accompanied by a bowl of the custard sauce.

Sauces

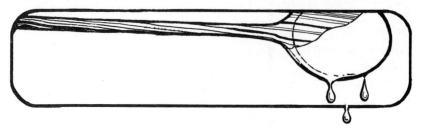

Caper Sauce

To make about 1 cup sauce

1 tablespoon butter
1 tablespoon flour
1 cup lamb, beef or fish stock,
depending on the food with which
it is to be served

1 tablespoon capers, drained and cut
into halves
2 teaspoons malt vinegar
¼ teaspoon salt
Freshly ground black pepper

In a heavy 8- to 10-inch skillet, melt the butter over moderate heat. When the foam begins to subside, stir in the flour and mix thoroughly. Pour in the stock and, stirring constantly with a whisk, cook over high heat until the sauce thickens and comes to a boil.

Reduce the heat to low and simmer the sauce for about 3 minutes to remove any taste of raw flour. Then stir in the capers, vinegar, salt and a few grindings of pepper. Taste for seasoning and serve hot from a small bowl or a sauceboat.

When made with the lamb stock, caper sauce traditionally accompanies boiled lamb. The beef-stock version would accompany boiled beef (*Recipe Index*) and other versions of this sauce, made with fish stock or even bottled clam juice, are served with boiled or poached fish, such as poached haddock (*Recipe Index*).

Mustard Sauce

To make about 1½ cups

2 tablespoons butter	1 teaspoon Dijon-style prepared
2 tablespoons flour	mustard
1 cup milk	1 teaspoon dry hot English mustard
4 tablespoons heavy cream	½ teaspoon salt
1 teaspoon distilled white vinegar	Freshly ground black pepper

In a heavy 6- to 8-inch skillet, melt the butter over moderate heat. When the foam subsides, stir in the flour and mix together thoroughly. Pour in the milk and, stirring constantly with a whisk, cook over high heat until the sauce thickens heavily and comes to a boil. Reduce the heat to low and simmer for about 3 minutes, then beat in the cream, vinegar, prepared mustard, dry mustard, salt and a few grindings of pepper. Taste for seasoning and serve at once.

Mustard sauce may be served with a variety of fish dishes including Finnan haddie (*Recipe Index*).

Egg Sauce

To make 1½ cups

2 hard-cooked eggs	1½ cups milk
2 tablespoons butter plus 1	1 tablespoon fresh lemon juice
tablespoon butter, softened	½ teaspoon salt
2 tablespoons flour	¼ teaspoon white pepper

Shell and separate the hard-cooked eggs. Chop the whites fine and with the back of a spoon rub the yolks through a sieve. Set them aside.

In a heavy 8- to 10-inch skillet, melt 2 tablespoons of the butter over moderate heat. When the foam begins to subside, stir in the flour and mix thoroughly. Pour in the milk and, stirring constantly with a whisk, cook over high heat until the sauce thickens heavily and comes to a boil. Reduce the heat to low, and simmer for about 3 minutes to remove any taste of raw flour. Stir in the lemon juice, salt and pepper, and then the eggs. Simmer for a minute or two and taste for seasoning. Just before serving, gently stir in the tablespoon of softened butter.

Egg sauce is traditionally served with poached or boiled fish, such as poached haddock (*Recipe Index*).

Horseradish Sauce

To make about 1 cup

¼ cup bottled horseradish, drained
  and squeezed dry in a kitchen
  towel
1 tablespoon white wine vinegar

1 teaspoon sugar
¼ teaspoon dry English mustard
½ teaspoon salt
½ teaspoon white pepper
½ cup chilled heavy cream

In a small bowl, stir the horseradish, vinegar, sugar, mustard, salt and white pepper together until well blended. Beat the cream with a whisk or a rotary or electric beater until stiff enough to form unwavering peaks on the beater when it is lifted from the bowl. Pour the horseradish mixture over the cream and, with a rubber spatula, fold together lightly but thoroughly. Taste for seasoning. Serve the sauce from a sauceboat as an accompaniment to roast beef (*Recipe Index*) or to such fish as smoked trout, smoked eel and grilled salmon.

Bread Sauce

To make about 2 cups

2 cups milk
5 tablespoons butter
1 small white onion, studded with
  2 whole cloves
1 small bay leaf
½ teaspoon salt

¼ teaspoon white pepper
3 cups fresh soft crumbs, made from
  homemade-type white bread,
  trimmed of crusts and pulverized
  in a blender or shredded with a
  fork
1 tablespoon heavy cream

In a heavy 2- to 3-quart saucepan, bring the milk, 4 tablespoons of the butter, onion, bay leaf, salt and pepper to a boil over moderate heat, stirring until the butter is completely melted. Set the pan aside off the heat and let the onion steep for 20 minutes, then discard it. Return the pan to moderate heat and bring the sauce to a boil. Gradually stir in the crumbs and cook, mashing them against the sides of the pan, until the sauce thickens and is somewhat smooth. Stir in the remaining 1 tablespoon of butter and the cream, and taste for seasoning. Serve at once. Bread sauce is traditionally served as an accompaniment to roast game birds such as pheasant (*Recipe Index*) and hot or cold roast chicken or turkey.

Cumberland Sauce

To make about 1 cup

1 medium-sized lemon
1 medium-sized orange
1 teaspoon sugar

⅓ cup port
2 tablespoons red currant jelly *(page 4)*
2 teaspoons cornstarch
1 tablespoon cold water

Using a small, sharp knife or rotary peeler, remove the skin of the lemon and the orange, being careful not to cut so deep as to include the bitter white pith.

Cut the lemon and orange peels into strips about 1 inch long and ⅛ inch wide and drop them into enough boiling water to cover them completely. Boil briskly, uncovered, for 5 minutes. Drain in a colander and run cold water over them to set their color. Set aside.

Squeeze the juice from the fruit into a small, heavy saucepan. Add the sugar, port and currant jelly, and bring to a boil over high heat, stirring until the jelly dissolves completely. Reduce the heat to low and simmer uncovered for about 5 minutes.

Dissolve the cornstarch in the tablespoon of cold water, and stir it into the simmering sauce. Cook, still stirring, until the sauce comes to a boil, thickens and clears. Strain the sauce through a fine sieve into a bowl. Stir in the lemon and orange peel and cool to room temperature. Then refrigerate until thoroughly chilled. Cumberland sauce is traditionally served with venison, ham and mutton.

Cumberland Rum Butter

To make about ¾ cup

4 tablespoons unsalted butter,
  softened
½ cup light-brown sugar, rubbed

through a sieve
¼ cup light rum
⅛ teaspoon ground nutmeg

Combine the butter, sugar, rum and nutmeg in a bowl, and beat with an electric beater until smooth and well blended. (By hand, cream the butter by beating and mashing it against the sides of a mixing bowl with a spoon until it is light and fluffy. Beat in the sugar, a few tablespoons at a time, and then the rum and nutmeg.) Refrigerate for at least 4 hours, or until firm. Cumberland rum butter is traditionally served with plum pudding *(Recipe Index)*.

Custard Sauce

To make about 1½ cups sauce

1½ cups milk

2 teaspoons cornstarch

1 tablespoon sugar

1 egg yolk

½ teaspoon vanilla extract

In a heavy 1- to 1½-quart saucepan, combine ¼ cup of the milk and the corn-starch, and stir with a whisk until the cornstarch is dissolved. Add the remaining 1¼ cups of milk and the sugar, and cook over moderate heat, stir-ring, until the sauce thickens and comes to a boil. In a small bowl break up the egg yolk with a fork and stir in 2 or 3 tablespoons of the sauce. Then whisk the mixture back into the remaining sauce. Bring to a boil again and boil for 1 minute, stirring constantly. Remove the pan from the heat and add the vanilla. Custard sauce is served hot with such desserts as blackberry-and-apple pie, apple dumplings or jam sponge *(for all, see Recipe Index)*.

Brandy Butter

To make about ¾ cup

4 tablespoons unsalted butter,
  softened

½ cup superfine sugar

3 tablespoons brandy

½ teaspoon vanilla extract

Combine the butter, sugar, brandy and vanilla in a bowl, and beat with an elec-tric beater until the mixture is smooth and well blended. (By hand, cream the butter by beating and mashing it against the sides of a mixing bowl with a spoon until it is light and fluffy. Beat in the sugar, a few tablespoons at a time, and continue beating until the mixture is very white and frothy. Beat in the brandy and vanilla.) Refrigerate at least 4 hours, or until firm. Brandy butter is traditionally served with plum pudding *(Recipe Index)*, and may be sprinkled with ground nutmeg before serving.

Recipe Index

NOTE: Size, weight and material are specified for pans in the recipes because they affect cooking results. A pan should be just large enough to hold its contents comfortably. Heavy pans heat slowly and cook food at a constant rate. Aluminum and cast iron conduct heat well but may discolor foods containing egg yolks, vinegar or lemon. Enamelware is a fairly poor conductor of heat. Many recipes therefore recommend stainless steel or enameled cast iron, which do not have these faults.

Fish

Meat, Poultry and Game

Savory Puddings and Pies

Sweet Puddings and Pies

Sauces

Notes

Drawings by Adrian Bailey.

Printed in U.S.A.